CUT IN HALF

Dear Sherry
Always Remember
Romans 8:38-39
Ana

CUT IN

HALF

HOW GOD MENDED ME
WITH 23 MIRACLES

ANA LE ROUX

Published by
Deep River Books
Sisters, Oregon
www.deepriverbooks.com

All Scripture verses are taken from the *King James Version* of the Bible unless otherwise noted.

ISBN: 1-935265-11-3
ISBN: 978-1-935265-11-5

Library of Congress: 2010922662

Printed in the USA

Cover design by Joe Bailen

*This book is dedicated to God,
all His angels, and all the people and situations on earth
He utilizes to show us His unconditional love.*

*"Give thanks unto the LORD, call upon his name,
make known his deeds among the people."*

1 Chronicles 16:8

INTRODUCTION

With God all things are possible
If only you believe
So may there be no limit
To the goals that you achieve

With God all things are possible
So may you always know
His loving care is guiding you
Wherever you may go

THESE WORDS APPEARED ON A HALLMARK CARD I RECEIVED FROM MY parents on the eve of a final exam. I was fifteen and convinced that the biggest test one can have in one's life was a difficult maths or science paper. Little did I know that these words would serve as a prophetic word for a test due to come my way fifteen years later.

It is very important to me that you identify with me. My goal is to show you that miracles happen every day in a variety of ways. You don't have to be ordained or blessed with a healing ministry to witness miracles. The only prerequisite is that you breathe. As long as you are in this world, you have a Saviour who longs to be at your beck and call.

I am not a pastor. I am not a gifted speaker. I am not even a writer. I am a sinner. Here is my story.

HOW THE BOOK WAS WRITTEN

This book is divided into three sections.

The *first* part of every chapter is the retelling of my story.

The *second* section is called the "Food for Thought" section. It is designed to help you reflect on the preceding story.

The *third* section is the "Soul Searching" section. I felt it necessary to include this into the book because I want to make you part of this experience. It is a chance for you to reflect on your own life and see all the wonderful things God has done for you too.

What I would like to have you take away from the "Soul Searching" section is twofold:

- It is important to me that you realize that the miracles you read about in this book are not limited to some stranger you've never met, but is a reality in your life every day.
- I would also like to dispel what I like to call myths. There are certain words, phrases, and clichés used in everyday life that diminish God's participation in everything you do: luck, coincidence, destiny, being at the right place at the right time. I am sure you can think of many more.

CHAPTER ONE

Because he hath set his love upon me, therefore will I deliver him: I will set him on high, because he hath known my name. He shall call upon me, and I will answer him: I will be with him in trouble; I will deliver him, and honour him. With long life will I satisfy him, and show him my salvation.

PSALMS 91:14–16

HI, I AM ANA LE ROUX. I AM A SOUTH AFRICAN LIVING IN NEW ZEALAND with my husband, Nico, and two children, Trinita and Christian. It is pretty remarkable that I am able to write this book. I was scheduled to die on the fifth of January 2003.

Nico, Trinita, and I immigrated to New Zealand in 2001. In early 2002 I became pregnant with Christian. The first year in a new country is usually desperately difficult for people, and we were no exception. As my pregnancy progressed and we started to feel more settled in our utopia, an overwhelming feeling of contentment came over us. Once Christian was there, our little family would be complete and all we had to do is look forward to our future in our new life.

Christian was born on the eleventh of December 2002. As far as childbirth goes, although very painful, it was a very blessed event. We had a 3.2 kg. healthy baby boy. I also bounced back remarkably soon after the birth. I had no pain, no bleeding, and no tearing. I felt great. My challenge now was to get settled into breastfeeding, something I really struggled with when Trinita was little.

We celebrated Trinita's third birthday on the fifteenth of December. A few days later my mum, who came over from South Africa for Christian's birth, suggested that she take little Trinita with her to Auckland to visit my brothers. That way I could get settled into breastfeeding without having to tend to a three-year-old. By this time Nico was on his Christmas leave and the two of us could spend all day bonding with our little bundle of joy. On the afternoon of the twenty-third, I started to feel a little flulike. By the evening, I had a 41°C temperature. Thankfully, a close friend of mine, Jeamien, who used to be a paramedic, stayed the night and helped Nico to help me fight the fever. The next morning Nico rang my midwife, who then insisted that I be hospitalized. I was diagnosed with double mastitis.

I was devastated. We were supposed to travel to Auckland on Christmas Eve. The thought of not spending Christmas with my little girl was very distressing. I was very ill and the doctors told me that I would have to remain in hospital until the twenty-seventh. My mum, worried sick and sensing my need to see Trinita, undertook the 150-km. drive with my brother, John, from Auckland to Hamilton on Christmas Day to visit me in hospital. It was then decided that Nico and I would drive up to Auckland as soon as I was released from the hospital. With the mastitis really taking its toll on my strength, being around the family over New Year's would give me more than enough babysitters while I regained my strength.

I must have had some kind of premonition, because I got an anxiety attack as we packed the car to travel northwards. I spent the whole trip silently praying, asking God to protect us. Having a two-week-old baby in the car does that to a new mum. We arrived at our destination safely.

Nico had to return to work on the fifth. Originally I was to stay on with my mum and the kids until the tenth. Soon after New Year's Day I started getting restless. I wanted to be at my home, in my bed, taking care of my kids. So when Nico started packing on Sunday morning, the fifth of January, I decided that I really wanted to go with him.

MIRACLE NO. 1

My mom did not travel with us. If she had, she would have sat in the seat that I was in when the accident occurred. I believe God wanted to spare her from an intense battle for survival. She was in her sixties and suffering from diabetes.

Why I classify this as a miracle is because my desire to be with-

out my mom was out of character for me. We are very close, and under any other circumstances I would insist my mom travel with us. That day I had an overwhelming desire to just be with Nico and the children.

After lunch we loaded the car. We pray before any long journey for God's protection, and this day was no exception. In our prayer we would always ask God to protect us with the promises in Psalms 91. Like many prayers repeated often, that request became habitual. I never really gave much thought to what actually stood in Psalms 91. I will now quote Psalms 91:15–16 to you, so please meditate on these words before continuing with me on my journey.

He shall call upon me, and I will answer him: I will be with him in trouble; I will deliver him, and honour him. With long life will I satisfy him, and show him my salvation.

It was a very hot summer's afternoon. I knew the children would get restless on a long trip in these temperatures. Christian, now twenty-five days old, had a feed before our departure. I knew, however, that he might require some water along the way. My first instinct was to sit in the middle backseat between both children in order to tend to their needs. But instead I got into the front passenger seat. About a half an hour into our trip, Christian became increasingly irritable. We decided to stop at a petrol station to stretch our legs and to get a refreshing drink. The fast-food restaurant at the petrol station was packed. We then realized that the majority of New Zealanders were heading back from their summer holiday to start work on the Monday morning.

After our little break, I told Nico that I should sit in the middle backseat. It would just make things easier and my presence would serve as a lot of comfort to the kids in these clammy circumstances. I got into the car and buckled up.

MIRACLE NO. 2

Nico hated wearing his safety belt. In all the years I knew him, he never put one on. It used to be a sensitive issue within our marriage. As he closed the car door, Trinita politely asked him to put on his seat belt. She had never asked him that before. He looked back at her and with a smile attempted some lame excuse as to why daddies don't need safety belts. Before he could open his mouth, however, he saw me glare at him. The type of glare a wife gives her husband to instill fear. Mumbling under his breath, he then reached for the belt and clicked it.

Within fifteen minutes of this happening, we had a serious head-on collision. The impact of which was more to the side that Nico was on. The lady directly opposite him in the other car did not wear her seat belt. She was flung through the windshield and passed away at the scene.

Now fully aware that his little girl had saved his life, he later asked her why she asked him to put his seat belt on. To which this little angelic three-year-old replied: "A little voice told me, daddy."

How awesome is our God? He uses anyone and everyone to fulfill His purpose, even little children who can hardly verbalize it yet.

This is what happened in the fifteen minutes leading up to the accident: It was between two and three in the afternoon when we pulled away from the petrol station. We needed to travel southward on State Highway 1 to reach our destination. The stretch of road from the center of Auckland southbound had double lanes for the first 70 km. Once one passed a town called Mercer, the road would narrow into single lanes. The road became increasingly curvy, and judging by all the white crosses flanking it, increasingly dangerous.

We only then realized how busy the road was that day. Suddenly, all we could see were cars everywhere. Our speed now decreased from 100km/h to 70km/h. All my focus was on giving Christian his water bottle. A few kilometers into this windy road, I heard a song playing on the radio. Earlier I told Nico about this new single by one of his favorite artists. When I heard the opening melody, I looked up at him to tell him to turn the volume up. The next few seconds were very surreal. It was one of those times in your life when the same amount of time feels like milliseconds and hours all at once. I saw a little red Toyota Starlet heading straight for us. My initial thought was that it was overtaking another vehicle, but Nico and I soon realized that the driver had no intention of moving back into his lane. Nico has incredible reflexes and immediately responded. We couldn't move right, because there was a long stream of cars. We couldn't move left because there was road construction. All Nico could do was brake and await our fate. Directly before impact, I stretched out my arms and braced the children. There was a very loud bang, then a palpable silence, followed by the deafening sound of children hysterically screaming.

At this point the shock had me numb. I just sat and stared in front of me. Nico turned around and asked me if I was all right. I told him that I didn't know. Just then I was hit by an intense pain. I started wailing and hyper-ventilating. He now knew something was seriously wrong with me. He got out of the car, his knees gushing blood, and attempted to tend to the children. Just then, two people rushed to his aid, a young man and woman. The woman, Meesha Geary, took Trinita and consoled her, while the man, Wayne Waysee, took Christian. Although I didn't see this, I know I would have found it tremendously endearing. Wayne was in his late teens, early twenties. It comes naturally to women to instinctively know how to help little ones in need. But here we had a young man, who, for all we knew, had never even held a baby before—not to mention, placate a very distressed newborn. Apparently Meesha and Wayne were able to settle the little ones down in a very short amount of time.

Nico's focus was now solely on me and God. He immediately started to pray out loud. I saw him pacing around the car in deep prayer, checking in on me every few seconds. He also immediately started texting and phoning everyone and begging them to pray for me. This vision of my husband, full of blood, in obvious pain, selflessly surrendering to God to help me, will always be one of my fondest memories.

It was chaos. The ambulances were there in minutes. The fire brigade were desperately trying to get the passengers of the other car out with the "jaws of life." There was blood all over that other car. Both passengers had been flung through the windshield of their car. The man was screaming in pain and I remember hearing the lady crying. I had no external injuries, so to the lay observer it looked like I was perhaps only in a state of shock. For this reason most people, and also the first medical personnel at the scene, went directly to help the occupants of the Starlet.

MIRACLE NO. 3

There was a lady in the car behind us who came to check on me. She had an incredible presence about her. She immediately made me feel at ease. She spoke calmly but with authority. She asked me where I had pain, felt my pulse, and gently stroked my arm. She was a nurse and her name was Loraine Abrahams. She knew I had internal injuries and suspected a fractured spine. She alerted the paramedics. Suddenly my right leg turned white as snow and she screamed out to the paramedics that I needed to be transported by helicopter and not by road.

You need to view this miracle in the context of when the accident took place. It was the last day of the summer holidays. This already busy stretch of highway, was experiencing its busiest day of the year. There were literally thousands of cars on that stretch of road. What are the odds of having an experienced nurse travelling directly behind you the day you have a horrific accident?

Loraine summoned a paramedic to start administering morphine. I was in excruciating pain. It was paramount that they keep me still as to not to aggravate any possible fracture I could have in my spine.

While Loraine was whispering encouragement to me, the paramedic pumped me full of morphine. The pain started subsiding and the drug had a calming effect. I was now ready for my first ever helicopter ride.

As you know, extreme care must be taken when a spinal or neck fracture is suspected. It took a lot of careful and deliberate handling of my body by the medical staff, to get me into the helicopter safely.

MIRACLE NO. 4

I only became aware of this significant miracle a few years after the accident. The helicopter was about to take off and the pilot had to confirm our destination. The accident occurred between two cities. The pilot had two options, as we were an equal distance away from two hospitals: Waikato Hospital in Hamilton and Middlemore Hospital in Auckland.

The voice on the other side of the two-way radio instructed the pilot to go to Waikato Hospital. The pilot started taking off. Just then, the voice retracted and said: "No, Middlemore Hospital, Middlemore Hospital!"

What is so remarkable about this is the nature of my injuries. It was extensive and it required specialist attention. I needed a very good abdominal surgeon and a very good cardio-vascular surgeon. I don't think the staff at Waikato Hospital was inferior to the staff at Middlemore. On the day, though, on call together, the best combination of brains to work on me were on call at Middlemore Hospital. The surgeon who mended my aorta, Mr. Adams, is thought to be one of the best in the country in his field. Prof. Martin, who worked on my abdominal injuries, heads the medical school at Auckland University. Many people have told me that I could not have been in better hands. I knew that to be true spiritually. Now it came as a great comfort to have it also be true physically.

Nico, Trinita, and Christian were taken to hospital via road ambulance. Nico was in a frantic emotional state, and although he would have wanted to escort me, his responsibility was now with the children. God was with him on that journey too. Within minutes of entering the ambulance, Christian drank his bottle and fell fast asleep, oblivious to anything going on around him. Trinita was also calm and intrigued by this strange vehicle they were in. Having the children act tranquilly, helped to center Nico. I think at that moment he grasped the severity of the situation.

Nico has often reflected back to that ride with awe. He says he knew that God was with the children. They were almost serenely calm. He didn't feel alone.

My recollection of the helicopter trip is a bit sketchy. I kept on dozing off. The man responsible for the accident lay across from me, savagely injured. His injuries were horrific. He moaned continuously. I was very worried about him.

The outstanding memory of my maiden helicopter voyage was the way the paramedic handled me. I know paramedics are trained for these situations, but his treatment of me was absolutely exceptional. He held me in his arms, encouraging me the whole time. He was a perfect stranger, yet he might as well have been a close relative by the way he appeased me. His empathy for my situation and his understanding of my mental state was so comforting.

The trip came to an abrupt end. Somehow I expected it to be longer. We were at Middlemore Hospital in a matter of minutes. The sight of someone being pushed through the ER with frantic hospital staff flanking the bed and the lights on the ceiling speeding by is familiar yet bizarre. It's a sequence of events most of us have seen in popular television shows or movies. When it is happening to you, though, it almost feels like an out-of-body experience. I once again lost consciousness momentarily. I woke up to the words: "Breathe in. And out." I was in the MRI scan. I got a few more requests from the radiology technician to breathe. I was then whisked off to the operating theater.

My last physical memory of the fifth of January 2003 was that of the anaesthetist telling me that I would get sleepy now...

FOOD FOR THOUGHT

God can use anyone, even three-year-olds!

Whether you are a Christian or not, if you are able to provide something for one of His children, He will utilize your gifts!

SOUL SEARCHING

When my mum was not invited to travel with us, it resulted in a minor argument. In retrospect we both know why I had the urge to go home alone. Has there ever been a time in your life where an argument or disagreement was followed by an incident that spiritually justified your standpoint?

We all have habitual prayers or memory verses that we recite. Sometimes we don't even give it much thought. Has there ever been a time in your life when a prayer or Bible verse became literal and you were made aware of it with a blinding realization?

God used Trinita to save her daddy's life. Can you recall a time God used an unlikely source to convey a message to you, and what was it?

Loraine Abrahams was a complete stranger who was utilized by God for my benefit. Has there ever been a time when a complete stranger seemed to be at the right place at the right time to help you?

Sometimes we are not aware of God's hand in certain things. I certainly didn't realize immediately that the choice between two hospitals would be so significant. Have you ever experienced a moment of: "That's why God let that happen!" What was it?

Have you ever heard a young child say something so profound that you almost feel guilty or even ignorant for not looking at the situation in the same way?

CHAPTER TWO

They that are whole have no need of the physician, but they that are sick: I came not to call the righteous, but sinners to repentance.

MARK 2:17

IN THIS CHAPTER IT IS ESSENTIAL TO DIVIDE EVENTS INTO THE PHYSICAL AND the spiritual. While the surgeons were meticulously trying to put my broken body back together, I was embroiled in a life-altering conversation with Almighty God.

IN THE PHYSICAL REALM

The X-rays revealed a very grim picture. The lap belt I was wearing *literally* cut my body in half. As the head-on collision occurred, my body jack-knifed. The force pulling me forward broke my spine, severed my aorta, and ripped through my colon and small intestines. With blood supply completely cut off from my legs, my legs were already dying.

While I was in radiology, Nico and the children arrived at the hospital. They were taken to the paediatric ER where the children were assessed. Both children were completely unharmed. Trinita had a little scratch over her shoulder, but it disappeared within twenty-four hours. Nurses also cleaned Nico's knees and diagnosed further action. During this time my mother arrived with my brother, John. The family had been enjoying afternoon tea with friends when they heard the news.

Desperate to know where I was and how I was doing, Nico and my mum proceeded to find out my fate. Nothing could prepare them for what the initial prognosis was.

My mother was introduced to Dr. Geller, the Intensive Care doctor on my case. He told her that I was in surgery and that my leg was being amputated. She was horrified, exclaiming that the surgeons must not go through with it. She pointed out that I would be unimaginably distressed if I should wake up with only one leg. Dr. Geller politely but sternly replied, "We are trying to save a life here; we are not concerned with the cosmetics. We must do what needs to be done."

That first surgery lasted between eight and nine hours. Hospital staff periodically came with updates, each one grimmer than the next. They stressed the seriousness of the injuries and the fact that no promises about my survival could be made.

By now my father and my in-laws were notified in South Africa and, along with thousands of other people, prayed for me to survive the night. While enduring the gruelling task of waiting for news, Nico carried on with his text prayer chain. I would later learn of people from all around the world responding to his prayer request. So, if you ever get an e-mail or text requesting a prayer for someone, leave everything you're doing and pray. It works!

The accident made news headlines in New Zealand. Initially, it was because of the sad passing of one of the occupants in the other car. Soon, however, the public became outraged that a young mother with a three-week-old baby had to fight for her life after sitting in a seat belt that had not been outlawed. A lot of awareness was raised about the dangers of lap seat belts and I am humbled that God would use me for such a potentially life-saving cause.

Although my mum and Nico were praying and trying to hope for a good outcome, the first night was desperately difficult for them and all my loved ones. They were given virtually no assurance that I would pull through. My mother in particular had a very difficult time. My one brother passed away at age twenty-nine. I was then three weeks shy of my thirtieth birthday. She was petrified that history could be repeating itself.

Sometimes I feel enormously guilty about those first forty-eight hours. I wish that I could have come out of the induced coma and told them that I was going to be all right. My husband and my parents endured a level of anguish I would not wish on anyone. Of everything that's happened the past five years, that is the thing I regret the most.

Their pain! The thought of it hurts to this day.

I survived the first night with my right leg intact. On Monday I needed more surgery. The surgery on Sunday was to stitch up my aorta and to remove the pieces of gut that were floating around in my belly.

MIRACLE NO. 5

If you think back to biology class: Your aorta is the main oxygen-carrying artery in your body. The lap belt ripped through a third of my aorta. I have not come across any doctor so far that has not been absolutely stunned that I am still around after such enormous trauma to the main "life giver" in my body.

To me this is symbolic of who the "real" giver of life is. Who really is in charge of the oxygen supply!

The surgery on Monday also lasted more than eight hours. Due to the severity of my injuries and the all-encompassing nature of it, it seemed like every time the surgeons thought they had everything under control, another life-threatening situation would present itself. On Monday evening my family was no closer to any reassurance. I was still critical. Another seemingly endless night awaited them.

I survived Monday night. The doctors had a better indication now of what was to be expected. My family was informed that I lost most of my colon, which meant that I would need to get rid of bodily waste through a bag. My back was broken. They were not able to fuse my spine and would wait until I was able to be laid on my stomach. It was, according to the surgeons, unlikely that I would walk again. The trauma also caused my kidneys to fail. I needed eight hours of dialysis a day. The surgeons also predicted that I would need more surgery in the upcoming days. The thing the surgeons feared most was the risk of infection. I managed to survive the first forty-eight hours, but the outlook of things to come was not very encouraging.

IN THE SPIRITUAL REALM

There are many documented cases of "near death" experiences out there. Most of them refer to people seeing a white light and then floating on top of the room. What I experienced was completely different.

Wherever I was, I was there with God and Satan. Or at least, I could feel Satan's presence. It was pitch black. I couldn't see anything; I could only hear voices. As the Bible teaches us:

> And I heard a loud voice in heaven, saying, "Now the salvation and the power and the kingdom of our God and the authority of his Christ have come, for the accuser of our brethren has been thrown down, who accuses them day and night before our God."

> REVELATION 12:10

I was on trial for my life. Satan was accusing me of not repenting all of my sins. There was one sin that I often did that I never asked for forgiveness. I led a relatively obedient life. I didn't drink or use drugs. I prayed every day of my life. I taught my daughter about Jesus. I tried not to gossip. I tried not to envy others. I was basically your run-of-the-mill follower of Christ. I was sinful and repentant all at the same time. The sin Satan was referring to, though, was something I had convinced myself was not a sin. I guess one can say I was in denial over it. I really thought it wasn't a big deal. So when this vision of this particular sin constantly was thrown at me, my initial reaction was: "You have got to be kidding me!" I soon realized that this wasn't exactly the right time to question God and Satan about their definition of sin.

You are really curious about what it was, aren't you? My husband worked in a professional sporting arena, surrounded by young, attractive, and athletic men. I really enjoyed looking at their physiques. In my mind I thought I was just appreciating their aesthetics, but Satan accused me of lustfully enjoying it. Replaying everything in my mind, I became so ashamed. I realized that he had a point. I felt appalled. I admitted to God that I knew it was wrong, and I apologized. From there on it was just the two of us. Satan backed off.

I introduced this chapter with Jesus' words: "They that are whole have no need of the physician, but they that are sick: I came not to call the righteous, but sinners to repentance." Physically, I needed a physician. If I did not repent that day, no physician could have saved me. I was spiritually very sick.

There are many religions out there and many "gods." What happened next is what, in my mind, sets my God above the rest. It proves that He is the One.

When God created us, he gave us freedom of expression and freedom of choice. Things would have been much easier for Him if he just forced us all to follow Him, no questions asked. He did not do that. He gave us all the ability to decide whether we want Him around or not. Is that not an ultimate mark of His respect for us?

Here I was fighting for my life and God asked me: "Do you want to carry on with your life on earth, or do you want to come with me?" Basically: "Do you want your body to live or die?"

Reflect on it for a minute. If you are asked right now by God whether you wanted to live or die, what would you respond? It's not exactly an easy question to answer, is it? Nevertheless, He still gave me the choice. I was in the worst place in my life; yet, He still trusted me to make a life-altering decision. To me that is not only a testimony of His love for us, but also His faith in us.

I told Him that I did not know. I said that the last memory I had of my children was of them screaming. I could not see any blood on them, but judging by my fate, I wasn't sure whether they had survived. I told God that if they had died, I wanted to die too and be with them in heaven. On the other hand, if they survived, I would like to raise them. In my mind it was a valid answer. God asked me again: "Do you want to live or die?" I remember becoming a bit annoyed and then repeating what I had said. God then asked me a third time: "Do you want to live or die?" I then shouted out: "I don't know!"

MIRACLE NO. 6

This debate seemed to have lasted for ages. Same question followed by the same answer, followed by the same question, then again followed by the same answer. Eventually, I felt really weary. I realized that He really needed an answer from me and I just couldn't give Him one. So I just said: "Please God, I trust you. Please make the decision for me?" Directly after making that request, I opened my eyes and saw Nico at my bedside.

The moral of the story: You are in charge of your own fate. Surrendering to God is also a choice. He will not force Himself on you. But the second you ask Him for help, He will jump in immediately and move mountains if He has to. Wow!

FOOD FOR THOUGHT

I would like to encourage anyone who has ever lost a loved one. Reuben Morgan and Darlene Zschech from Hillsong Church in Sydney, Australia, composed a popular song called "At the Cross." This song was dedicated to a member of their church who died very young. The last verse says: "And when the earth fades. Falls from my eyes. And You stand before me, I know You love me. I know You love me!" It is absolutely, undeniably true. While the living and healthy are in torment over the physical state of a loved one in hospital or at an accident scene, the sick or dying person is with God. They can feel His love. They are in the best place they had ever been before.

God is the God of second chances! The next words were written by the apostle Paul. He was on "death row." Nero was about to execute him.

For I am already on the point of being sacrificed; the time of my departure has come. I have fought the good fight, I have finished the race, I have kept the faith.

2 TIMOTHY 4:6–7

At the time of the accident, I was a practicing Christian. I led a life I deemed necessary to fulfill God's Word. In reality, it was all about me. I lead a life of me, myself, and I. I had not fought the good fight. I had not finished the race with a satisfactory placement. I had not kept the faith.

But God is the God of second chances. When God was asked by thousands of people to save my life, He answered their prayers. He gave me a reprieve. Now I wish to bring to fruition the next words of Paul:

> But the Lord stood by me and gave me strength to proclaim the message fully, that all the Gentiles might hear it. So I was rescued from the lion's mouth.
>
> 2 TIMOTHY 4:17

I want everyone to know about the love of God!

> And you, being dead in your sins and the uncircumcision of your flesh, hath he quickened together with him, having forgiven you all trespasses; Blotting out the handwriting of ordinances that was against us, which was contrary to us, and took it out of the way, nailing it to his cross.
>
> COLOSSIANS 2:14

God forgives and forgets. I wasn't held accountable for any other sins than the one I hadn't yet repented of. During my life I had committed terrible sins. I repented all of them, but somehow, being hard on myself, I expected to give reckoning for those events as well. I wasn't! As far as God was concerned, it was already dealt with.

SOUL SEARCHING

If you have a mobile phone and access to the Internet, you have undoubtedly on occasion received prayer request texts or e-mails. Do you respond?

Has there ever been an occasion where you have responded with a little prayer and later learned that the person survived, or was healed, or a favorable outcome was achieved?

Do you believe in the power of prayer? In detail, write down your fondest memory of an answered prayer.

It is often said that there are only three answers to prayer: Yes, No, and I have something better in mind. Recall a time where you thought that a prayer went unanswered, just to realize that God had something better in mind.

Although I suffered immense injury, God was able to use the publicity of the tragedy to potentially save lives. My case is extreme, but has there ever been a time that God used an apparent tragedy in your life to create awareness of something in the lives of others?

In modern society we believe that knowledge is power. We also put a lot of emphasis on logic. I spent three years at a university learning about the human body. My surgeons all spent in excess of seven years studying the workings of, in my opinion, God's most awesome masterpiece; humans. Yet, God can defy our logic, and bring into question our knowledge, by a single inexplicable act. Has there ever been a time in your life where what you "know" as true and "factual" was brought into question because God intervened?

Is there a habitual sin in your life that you are in denial about? It's usually something that deep down you know is not right, but you justify it by what society deems acceptable. What is it? What can you do stop the behaviour or thought? Take a minute to repent and ask God for forgiveness.

During my conversation with God, I really wanted Him to make the decision for me. Have you ever been in a very difficult situation or circumstance and you knew that God had all the answers, and all you wanted was for Him to make the decision for you? What was it? What was the outcome? What did you learn from that experience?

We are creatures created with a free will. We all have a conscience and we all intrinsically know right from wrong. We are also on occasion stubborn creatures, trying to force our will on others. Have you ever tried to force your will on God? What was the outcome?

Did you learn that surrendering your will to God will result in a more favorable outcome?

Has there ever been a decision in your life that required of you to surrender your will to God? What was it?

CHAPTER THREE

"Eli, Eli, la'ma sabach-tha'ni?" that is, "My God, my God, why hast thou forsaken me?"

MATTHEW 27:46

I FEEL VERY APPREHENSIVE ABOUT RETELLING THE EVENTS THAT FOLLOW. I must now go to memories of my ordeal that I have spent a great deal trying to forget. Here is my account of my two weeks in the Intensive Care Unit. I am telling it from my perspective. Some of it my recounting not be factually accurate, but it is how I remember it.

I awoke after two days. It was now the seventh of January. Over the next eight days I went through undoubtedly the darkest time of my life, hence the above quote: "My God, my God, why hast thou forsaken me?" During this time, I was constantly in a drug-induced daze. I had more surgery on the ninth. The little portion of my colon that the surgeons were able to save on Sunday was now infected and poisoning my system. I was also constantly having a variety of tests done, and although I can't remember it, I know that I visited the operating theater more than once between the ninth and the sixteenth of January.

On about the third day I had trouble breathing, and my nurse spent the whole day desperately trying to keep me breathing. She was extremely tired and emotionally drained by the end of the day. The doctors wanted me to start breathing on my own and I had trouble doing that, constantly gasping for the oxygen mask. I remember that same nurse taking me for a follow-up MRI scan. Anyone who has had an MRI scan before would know that it can be a bit claustrophobic at best. I had to stay still in this chamber for thirty minutes not being able to breathe properly. Needless to say, it was frightening and luckily I passed out. When I awoke the next day I was able to breathe more readily.

For the first time, I started becoming aware of my surroundings. I told my mother that I wanted to see the children. I was convinced that they were lying to me when they said the children were fine. I also thought I had a maimed face. I was torn in two. I desperately wanted to see the children, but I didn't want to scare them. I knew in my soul, they were the key to me fighting this, but at the same time I didn't know how I would deal with it if the worst had happened. It was torture.

Unbeknown to me, a major debate erupted around this same issue. My mum and my sisters-in-law felt it would be good if I saw the children. Being mothers themselves, they understood exactly where I was coming from. Nico and my brothers felt that it would be too traumatic for Trinita to see me that way. An argument ensued, but eventually my children were brought in. I took one look at them and it confirmed to me that God made the decision for me. That was the single most significant event in determining how I was going to deal with this situation. I no longer felt that God had forsaken me. He spared my husband and my children. My challenge now was to get well.

As far as ICU patients go, I was very demanding, to say the least. I would not allow a nurse or doctor near me without them giving me a full and accurate explanation of what they were about to do and why. I even wanted to know the dosage of medication, its side effects, and any alternatives. For someone barely aware of my surroundings, I was a huge pain in the behind. Luckily, the staff found my behavior more endearing than annoying.

In a normal hospital ward, a nurse would have a shift of eight hours, sometimes twelve. In ICU, nurses have twelve-hour shifts and they are responsible for only one patient at a time. One day I was assigned a young male nurse. Up until then I had the same two ladies during the day shift. My mind, playing tricks on me, convinced me that this nurse was the Devil and his sole purpose was to kill me. I went into an irrational tirade, begging Nico to get someone else to look after me. He tried hard to put me at ease, but I wouldn't hear of it. This nurse had to go! The way Nico handled this situation and many more erratic outbursts is commendable. He had his hands full with me. Usually, I am a very rational and cooperative person. This feisty and demanding diva he was keeping a vigil with must have frightened the living daylights out of him.

The most difficult thing to endure during the first eleven days was being moved. I still had not had my back surgery. The nurses had to move me twice a day to prevent bed sores from forming. Nico was there most of the time. My nurse, Nico, and six other nurses would gather around my bed, and with military precision they would prepare to move me without in any way moving my spine. I honestly don't have enough adverbs in my vocabulary to accurately convey the amount of pain this caused. With the memory of natural childbirth relatively fresh in my mind, I had something to compare this pain to. I would have faced childbirth any day if I could be guaranteed that I didn't need to be moved.

I am sure my heart monitor clearly showed my distress every time the nurses gathered around my bed. I had a handheld pain dispenser. I pressed it so many times it looked more like I was playing Play Station than pumping myself full of morphine. The drugs did nothing to numb the pain. I soon realized the only one who could help me get through this suffering was God.

I recalled a sermon I heard on television once. I couldn't remember who spoke those words, but it occurred to me that I needed to do what he had suggested. The pastor said that if you only prayed one prayer in your life, it had to be a prayer of thanksgiving. I decided that the next time I saw the nurse's approach, I would drug myself and start praising God for getting me through those excruciating sixty seconds. All I did was repeat the words: "Thank you, Jesus; thank you, Jesus!"

Praising God did not ease the pain, but it got me through the pain. There are times in your life when you just wish God would take away a burden. Many times He does, but when there are times that He doesn't, calling out to Him is not in vain. It is never in vain. The burden will still be there, but your companion during this time will make light weight of an otherwise impossible situation.

As a result of that experience, praising God has become an integral part of my daily life. I truly believe it is impossible to thank God enough for all the blessings he gives you every day. I also believe that when I thanked Jesus, I acknowledged that although I was in the darkest time of my life, I was eternally grateful that He was my best friend.

I was scheduled to have two more procedures: the fusion of my spine and a fasciotomy on the wound on my right leg. Unfortunately, the surgeons due to perform these surgeries had clashing schedules. So I had to have the fasciotomy on the sixteenth and the fusion on the seventeeth. The doctors at the ICU were very troubled by this. They had hoped that I could be anesthetised once and have both procedures done in one day. They were very concerned that I would have so many surgeries in such a short amount of time. Minimizing my exposure to the anesthetic was crucial. Their concerns were soon vindicated. The night of the sixteenth I became delirious.

Somehow the medication in my system in conjunction with the anesthetic started me off on a seemingly endless hallucination. It was the strangest experience of my life. It consisted of different sequences of events flashing through my memory. Some were actual memories, some were random colors, shapes, or images, but most were incomprehensible, illogical events. One such event was a baby running naked on the ceiling of the ICU.

Across from me there was an elderly man covered in dry blood. The nurses were putting leeches on him to extract the excess blood. During my delirium I kept on feeling these leeches eating at my leg. For days I believed I was covered in leeches. It was dreadful! I had never in my life taken hallucinogenic drugs and after my experience that night I honestly don't know why anyone would willingly do so.

MIRACLE NO. 7

The nurse must have given me something to help me sleep because the next time I woke up it was after my fusion, twenty-four hours later. My spine was now fused, yet I still expected it to be painful when moved. I lay there waiting for the nurses, psyching myself up for the linen change. As they approached, I closed my eyes and started thanking Jesus. They lifted me and… nothing! No pain! None whatsoever! A complete one-hundred-eighty-degree shift. It has been six years since the accident, and the sixteenth of January 2003 was the last day I had pain in my back. Hallelujah!

Next to the man being treated with leeches was another elderly man suffering from emphysema. Although I couldn't see him, I heard him gasping for air all the time. My heart went out to him because he was in obvious despair. The sad thing about his predicament was that he was ill because of cigarettes, yet he now had an overwhelming desire for a "fix." The thing that brought him there was the one thing he wanted. It reminded me of how cruel Satan was and how much I needed Jesus.

I also had kidney failure and was receiving eight hours of dialysis a day. Under normal circumstances dialysis would only have a mild level of discomfort. My dialysis was very painful. I don't have a medical explanation for it, but my best uneducated guess was that it was due to the extensive swelling in my body. In essence, dialysis is the recycling of blood through a machine where it is 'cleaned'. The swelling probably made the circulation a bit tardy. All I know is that I dreaded those eight hours.

By now I was very alert and able to sustain a logical conversation. Every time I asked for water, the nurse would dip some water in cotton wool and dab it on my lips. This, being my first ICU experience, I assumed was how all ICU patients got their thirsts quenched. As the days went by and I was able to verbalize my needs more readily, I started telling them that I needed more water. I was very, very thirsty. During the rounds one morning, the nurses had the renal specialists explain to me why I could only get a little dabbed water on my lips. My kidneys weren't working at all, so I wasn't able to urinate. I was allowed 100 ml. of fluid an hour. That did not quite cut it for me. We were in the middle of summer, I had a high fever, and to top it all off, my bed caught the afternoon sun. I was desperate for water. It may seem hard to believe, but my overwhelming thirst was by far my worst experience in ICU. For almost everything else there was a drug that could lessen the full effect of a treatment or symptom. No medical practitioner, however, could prescribe me something that could help mobilize the excess water in my system. I had to remain thirsty; there was simply nothing they could do.

My husband had a meeting with one of the renal specialists. She informed him that my kidneys might start working in about eight to ten months. She suspected they would never function as before. Nico's task was now to prepare me mentally for a lifetime of dialysis.

By the thirteenth day after the accident, the eighteenth of January, my longing for something to drink reached its pinnacle. Every few minutes I would summon a different nurse or doctor to my bed and attempt to bribe them into quenching my thirst. I was experiencing a level of extreme anxiety I never knew humanly possible. My mind understood why the doctors couldn't give in to my demands, but my body rebelled.

It is often told that a human can go without food for extended periods of time, but can perish if water is withheld for only a few days. This reminded me of Jesus' words about the living water. It only then dawned on me that he didn't liken it to living food, but living water.

> *Jesus answered her, "If you knew the gift of God, and who it is that is saying to you, 'Give me a drink,' you would have asked him, and he would have given you living water."*

> JOHN 4:10

It was evening. The lights were turned off. I'd already bribed, begged, demanded, and threatened everyone there. I decided it was now time to beg God for the living water. I prayed and asked God if He could overflow me with living water. I told Him that I understood my physical predicament, but in my heart I knew that His living water could quench all that needed to be quenched. Just then I became drunk with the Holy Spirit. I was overcome with so much force and deliberate caressing, it completely overwhelmed me. I started laughing out loud. I couldn't stop laughing. My nurse became so annoyed with me she yelled at me to be quiet. I continued laughing with joy. I started talking out loud about how wonderful God was for saving my life and healing me. The nurse thought I was once again delirious and summoned the doctor. When he came to my bedside, I pulled him closer and gave him a big hug and a kiss on the cheek. I then proceeded to tell him about my joy over what God was doing. He smiled uncomfortably and nodded in agreement. He also then asked me to please keep it down. He said that I was being inconsiderate to all the other patients. I heeded to his request and continued my drunken escapade in the silence of my heart.

FOOD FOR THOUGHT

That night God taught me a very important lesson: *When you are at your weakest, God is at His strongest!* I was lying in the Intensive Care unit. I'd undergone numerous surgeries in a short time frame. I hadn't eaten in two weeks. I was weak with thirst. I was paralyzed. I hardly had the strength to lift my head. But that night I could've conquered the world.

I also learned that thankfulness and gratitude bring blessings. When you are in the midst of trials and tribulations and manage to face it with a thankful heart, you are honoring God. You are showing Him that you believe that He is in control. It is a selfless act of love.

SOUL SEARCHING

Have you ever thought about the importance of praise, especially in seemingly hopeless circumstances?

It is easy to praise God when things are going well, and you should.

But it is even more critical to do so when things are not that rosy. Recall a time in your life where praising God in that circumstance was the very last thing you *felt* like doing.

Try to visualize what the outcome could have been had you praised God then against the odds. Do you think the outcome might have been more favorable?

The principle of relentless praise comes down to love, respect, and trust. When you praise God in every circumstance, you are telling Him that you love, respect, and trust Him enough to help you regardless of the situation you find yourself in. If you feel you are not at that point yet spiritually, write down an action plan of how you will approach the next difficult challenge in your life.

CHAPTER FOUR

And Jesus said to him, "All things are possible to him who believes."

MARK 9:23

"Truly, I say to you, whoever says to this mountain, 'Be taken up and cast into the sea,' and does not doubt in his heart, but believes that what he says will come to pass, it will be done for him."

MARK 11:23

IT WAS NOW SUNDAY THE EIGHTEENTH OF JANUARY. I AWOKE TO THE CHEERY face of my daytime nurse. She excitedly told me about a brainstorm she had during the night.

MIRACLE NO. 8

She told me that she couldn't stop thinking about my intense thirst. She knew that it had to have been terrible. During the course of the night it suddenly dawned on her that if I sucked an ice block every hour, it could help. Not only did the ice block contain less than 100ml of fluid, but the cold temperature could help alleviate my fever. When she spoke these words I knew God had given her this brainstorm. The time she claimed to have thought of this corresponded with the time the Holy Spirit was feeding me with "living water."

Nico rushed to the cafeteria and bought a few ice blocks. I would open one on the hour, every hour, and leisurely suck on it. During the course of the day my thirst started subsiding. My desperation was replaced with excitement.

My brother John brought my children in to see me in the afternoon. Trinita's face was imprinted in my memory but I couldn't remember what Christian looked like. Not remembering his sweet little face made me feel like I was a terrible mother. My mind simply could not recall what he looked like.

When I eventually saw him, he looked completely different to what I remembered. I immediately felt a sense of loss. I lost two weeks of his life. He was unrecognizable to me. It was as if he was simply a baby who came to visit me. It didn't feel like he was mine. When they left I started sobbing uncontrollably. I realized that any bonding that occurred between the two of us was now gone. What if he forgot that I was his mommy?

Soon after they left I had already forgotten what he looked like. I begged Nico and my mum to please bring in photos of him and Trinita the next day. What kind of mother could not remember what her children looked like? At that point I wasn't aware that my memory lapses were due to all the anesthetic. In retrospect, I think I was pretty hard on myself. I was convinced I was a bad mother.

I was not only beating myself up about that. There were two other things weighing heavily on my mind. My father had already been in New Zealand for a week. He kept a vigil next to my bed, and his presence meant the world to me. I knew, however, that he had work commitments and that he would have to return back to South Africa soon. I knew that I couldn't keep him near me. That really hurt. It cut deep into my core.

Another source of emotional pain was not seeing my brother Ronnie. All families have their disagreements and in extreme cases even feuds. Ours is no different. For a few years leading up to the accident, three of my brothers were embroiled in a feud, resulting in Ronnie cutting himself off from the family.

I really wished that my situation would encourage them to bury the hatchet. It didn't. All I wanted was a visit from my brother. I believed that he didn't want to see me and he believed that I didn't want to see him. So, we both fell into the trap of naively believing the Devil's lies. (Thankfully, God has worked hard with us since to restore our relationship!)

The emotional weight of the situation slowly presented itself that day. I was faced with a conundrum. For the first time in two weeks things were looking up physically, but the sadness I was feeling completely overshadowed any strides I had made. Reality was quickly sinking in.

The next morning I was visited by Dr. Stephan Joubert. He was a minister at a South African congregation in Auckland. He periodically visited me during the preceding two weeks; this was, however, the first time that I could communicate with him lucidly. He told me about an experience he had the first night he saw me: He had looked down at my broken body and asked God for strength, as he was sure I was not going to make it. He needed the strength to comfort my family. As he turned to exit the ICU, God gave him a vision of a jigsaw puzzle and told him that He was going to heal me piece by piece.

Stephan's words were very comforting. I asked him if he could gather my parents and Nico around my bed and pray for me. Matthew 18:19 says: "Again I say unto you, That if two of you shall agree on earth as touching any thing that they shall ask, it shall be done for them of my Father which is in heaven." My request was specific. He had to ask God to heal my kidneys. The four of them took hands and started to pray. It was a very simple prayer. Stephan thanked God for bringing me through the first two weeks and then pleaded with God to heal my kidneys.

I then did what Jesus instructed: "Truly, I say to you, whoever says to this mountain, 'Be taken up and cast into the sea,' and does not doubt in his heart, but believes that what he says will come to pass, it will be done for him." I believed with every fiber in my being that my kidneys would start working.

A few hours after the prayer, I felt the need to urinate. I informed the nurse that I wet the bed. She checked and my bed was dry. It was recorded in my notes. The renal specialists promptly let the intern on duty know that it was normal to have a need to urinate. It was not in any way indicative of my kidneys coming back to life. Over the next three days it constantly felt like I'd wet the bed. I'd summon the nurse just to have her tell me the bed was dry.

I left ICU the same day as the prayer, Monday the twentieth. I was now in the orthopedic ward. I still needed my dialysis, but now had to be taken to the renal ward to receive it. In the renal ward the nurse assigned to me was a miniscule Asian lady who was seven months pregnant. During those eight hours it felt like I'd wet the bed at least five times. She couldn't lift me to check and even if she could, she probably wouldn't, because she believed that it was simply a reflex. By this time I was giving my testimony to everyone I came into contact with. I spent those eight hours telling all the nurses of the work God was doing in my life.

MIRACLE NO. 9

Once back in the ward, I asked my nurse, Shandra, to humor me and look if my bed was wet. She sighed and reluctantly lifted my sheet, expecting to find it perfectly dry. It was sopping wet!

She fitted a catheter and informed the renal unit. The next morning I had to undergo a few tests and scans. In the afternoon, the specialist on my case entered my room. She was a strikingly beautiful Middle-Eastern lady in her Muslim attire. She started to convey to me the results of the tests. As she was doing this, she got tears in her eyes. She told me that my kidneys were flawlessly healthy and functioning normally. I just smiled and told her that I asked God to heal me and He had.

It was by now incontestable that God was in charge. This unfortunately meant that Satan had to try and intervene. The first twenty-four hours in the ward was tremendously difficult for me. I was very paranoid. I didn't see my nurse wash her hands and that sent me into a panic attack. She did wash her hands, but I chose to believe otherwise. I kept on telling everyone that I'd fought hard to be here and I didn't want to risk infection. I was frantic. Later that evening I had another bout of hallucinations. I thought the fact that I couldn't get up was because of chains to my hands and feet, not my paralysis. I would periodically wake up and start screaming. It took Nico and four nurses to pin me to the bed. I constantly ripped off all the IVs and insisted that Nico and I flee this place we were kept captive. Nico later realized that I would space out if Tramadol and morphine were combined as pain relief. The doctors altered this and that was the end of my unpredictable behavior. At least for now...

When night fell I would get uneasy and insisted the lights stayed on. I found that I was uncharacteristically afraid of the dark. This went on for four nights. On the fifth night my fear escalated to a point where I experienced terror. I soon realized that it was Satan trying to intimidate me. I knew I had to fight fire with fire. I pressed the buzzer, and when the nurse arrived, instead of asking her to turn on the main light, I asked her to tune my radio in to a Christian radio station. I knew the sound of praise and worship would chase away any unwelcome presence in my room. As the nurse tuned the radio, we started talking. She told me she was a Christian too. I gave her my testimony and we chatted for about a half an hour. She had trouble setting the radio. She told me that she had to run out quickly but that she'd be back soon. After about twenty minutes, she returned to my bed with three tapes. She had gone down to her car to get gospel tapes for me to listen to. I was very appreciative but didn't know how I would get the tapes back to her. She gave me her name and mobile number and said that once I was done with them, she'd be back to pick them up.

MIRACLE NO. 10

After a few weeks I rang her to pick up the tapes. The person at the other end informed me that I had the wrong number. At the time I thought nothing of it, but as time went by I realized Maree's presence that night was also a miracle. I spent over twelve weeks in the hospital. When you're there for that long, you get to know all the nurses, orderlies, and administrative staff in your ward. I always had the same nurses, with the exception of Maree. It has been suggested to me that Maree could have been an angel helping me out that night. That is possible.

It doesn't matter if Maree was a human or an angel; her presence that night was another miracle. Not only was conversing with her comforting to me, but the music she gave sent any evil in my room packing. Whatever it was that was scaring me before, it disappeared as I listened to "Shout to the Lord" over and over again.

FOOD FOR THOUGHT

If you ask God for something and not doubt it in your heart, it will be done. It is something I'd read many times before, but I had a hesitant heart. I doubted God many times in my life. If I had listened to His promises before, who knows how many prayers, that I had deemed unanswered, could have come to fruition?

SOUL SEARCHING

The nurse had an epiphany about how to remedy my thirst. In my heart I knew the "brainstorm" came directly from God. Have you ever been confronted by a person with help or advice without you asking for it, yet knowing it was God who sent them on your path? What were the circumstances and how did that person help you?

Matthew 18:19 says: "Again I say unto you, That if two of you shall agree on earth as touching any thing that they shall ask, it shall be done for them of my Father which is in heaven" (King James). Other translations do not mention "touching any thing," but I really like this image of two or more believers by faith being able to simply touch something to make a miracle happen. Do you ever ponder the unlimited and supreme power of faith? Do you really believe in its existence? Take a moment to ask God for that kind of unrelenting faith.

In the current global political climate we are overshadowed by fundamentalist terrorism. How has it affected your view of your neighbor? What do you think and feel when you encounter a Muslim person? Does the principle of "Love thy neighbour" still apply, or have you allowed your judgement to be clouded by politics?

Have you ever been in a situation where you have experienced unjustifiable fear or anxiety? Have you perhaps felt an uncharacteristic fear of the dark at some stage? What did you do to remedy the situation?

God sent Maree to help me cope with the Devil's attack that night. Have you ever had a stranger or an unlikely visitor show up exactly "at the right time" during a crisis in your life? Who was it, and how did their presence alleviate the situation?

We are all human and we all doubt. Jesus was very firm about asking and then uncompromisingly believing that it would be done. What can you do to your mindset to allow your doubts to subside?

Chapter Five

For we walk by faith, not by sight.

2 Corinthians 5:7

In the above verse, Paul was not referring to literal walking, but more a journey in faith. It is a journey I endeavor to live by too. The events that follow, though, give the above verse a whole new dimension. It became literal to me.

My injuries were too extensive and severe for the doctors to handle every injury and subsequent outcome simultaneously. Because a variety of functions were affected, I was overseen by doctors from various fields. As my condition stabilized in a more critical area, the doctors would tick it off and start focusing on the next level of concerns.

I was now in the orthopedic ward, and the main focus was the healing of my spine. Nico was told that it was very likely that I would be paralyzed for life.

It did not cross my mind once that I could be paralyzed. I knew in my heart that I wasn't. I believed that God granted me my second chance to be the mother I was meant to be. I couldn't be that mother from the confines of a wheelchair. I'd always been an active person, joining my daughter on the playground and jumping with her on the trampoline. I couldn't be *me* without my legs functioning as before. So, possible paralysis was simply a nonissue for me. I was convinced God needed me to walk and that was exactly what I was going to do.

For the first two weeks in the ward, various doctors would periodically perform the ASIA test. It is a test developed specifically to assess a person's level of paralysis. I constantly 'failed' the test, increasing the likelihood of long-term paralysis. Even during those times, I didn't budge in my convictions. I was going to walk again.

I told Nico that we were going to walk on the beach in December. I could see the four of us strolling along the surf.

I suspect people around me thought that I was in denial about my fate. They probably thought that I didn't want to face the inevitable. They were going by sight, not faith!

During the third week in the ward, I was visited by a spinal specialist, Dr. Ackland. He flew in from Christchurch bi-weekly to visit patients at the spinal unit, a facility for the disabled. The purpose of his visit was to ascertain the level of intervention I needed in order for the spinal unit to accommodate me. He once again performed the ASIA test and also requested a few additional movements. After his consultation, he assured me that I would walk again. Although I knew it in my heart, I felt incredibly vindicated having it confirmed medically.

At that point I had already undergone hours of physiotherapy. His new prognosis meant that my treatment could now be streamlined and any goals could be redefined. Every morning at ten a.m. the physiotherapists would visit my room. I was still very weak and dependant on intravenous feeding, so I had to have treatment in there. My progress was painfully slow. Sensing my frustration, my physiotherapist, Sheralata, suggested I keep a diary. It was a great idea. As the weeks flew by, reading about my progress over time was a huge motivating factor in itself.

Entry of the seventeenth of February: Sheralata and Jos, her assistant, used a tilting bed to get me upright. I'd been lying down for forty-two days. Being tilted vertically rushed blood down to my feet and I found the whole experience agonizing and nauseating.

Entry of the twelfth of March: I attempted standing exercises. While contracting my gluteus muscles, I bent my knees and swayed from left to right.

Every day I came a bit closer to my goal of taking that illusive first step.

At my university, one of my majors was physiology. It was a subject I found profoundly interesting, but up until that point, had not used it in my career. The knowledge of my body became invaluable during the three months in hospital. I was paralyzed from the waist down. I couldn't move. There were very slight twitches, but other than that, there was no movement.

I knew that if I stimulated the muscles in my legs constantly, forcing blood supply to the areas, the oxygenation would help with regenerating things. I set about "training" for six to seven hours a day. My workout would start at eight a.m. I had an electric massager. I would massage each leg for an hour. At ten I would have my physiotherapy session. It lasted between forty-five minutes and an hour. From eleven to one, I had my legs put on a machine that would mechanically move them in circular motions. I usually took a little nap and spent another two hours on the machine in the late afternoon. Not only did this routine give me some structure to my day, but it provided me with a purpose. I spent most of the three months in the hospital in isolation, due to a bacterial infection I attracted. Without company, the days tended to drag on. My workouts were an important part of my keeping my sanity.

Undoubtedly, the most important aspect of my regaining my mobility was my unwavering faith that I would walk again. That faith drove and inspired me. My level of commitment would not have been possible had I not known of God's commitment to see me through this experience. I wanted to walk for Him.

During the same week of Dr. Ackland's visit, I was introduced to food. Up until that point the only thing to pass my lips was fluid. During the second day of eating, my nurse and I noticed a strange smell coming from my abdominal area. Upon closer examination, it was revealed that the food I was consuming; was immediately trickling out of my many open abdominal wounds. It was not a pretty sight. My nurse had to leave the room. She was white as snow. I can only speculate what she went to do. The orthopaedic specialists decided that it would be better if I be transferred to the surgical ward. Professor Martin oversaw everything there and he would be better equipped to deal with my severe abdominal trauma.

My body was obviously not ready to deal with the task of digestion. I was banned from food until further notice. I visited radiology. There a technician inserted a minute tube into my left arm. This tube was navigated via my shoulder to the artery connecting with my heart. This tube would deliver my food source for the next two months. My nutrition was called TPN. It was administered via IV into the tube. Every morning a phlebotomist would draw some blood. That blood would then be analyzed and a balanced substance would be formulated and delivered to the ward at six p.m. The "food" was photosensitive and had to be covered at all times. Inside this bag were all the proteins, carbohydrates, lipids, vitamins, and minerals my body needed for the next twenty-four hours. It was so well balanced that I never once felt hungry. All my nutritional needs were met.

With the TPN now bypassing my digestive system, the doctors were focusing on healing the holes in my abdomen. I initially had four fistulas. All that really could be done was keep them clean and wait for them to heal.

The process of waiting for the fistulas to heal became the most challenging experience in hospital. It delayed everything. Had I not had these fistulas, I probably could've left the hospital the first week of February. I stayed there until the eleventh of April.

FOOD FOR THOUGHT

When you ask God for something, faith in its eventuating is only part of the process. You need to work at things at your end too. If I had lain in my bed and simply waited for my legs to regain their strength, it would have undermined my commitment to my goal. I knew that I had to do everything I could from my end to help the process along.

I am not implying that God won't answer your prayer if you wait passively in faith. I just think that when you combine your faith with the active pursuit of your goal it makes the attaining of it sweeter. It is a group effort, between you and God.

SOUL SEARCHING

I knew in my heart that God did not bring me back to earth to be anything less than what I was. I also knew that in order for me to reach my full potential and purpose I had to believe that God could heal me completely. How do you view yourself and your purpose in this life as an employee, a spouse, a parent, a child? How do you think your view of your life and purpose differs from God's view of you?

I never intended to major in physiology. It is something that came across my path and for a long time remained a mystery to me. I enjoyed my studies, but felt for a long time that all the knowledge I acquired was in vain, as I did not have a job in which to utilize it. But, my knowledge of the human body became invaluable during my recovery. Have you ever done something or experienced something that did not make sense at the time, but later on became significant? What was it?

CHAPTER SIX

Therefore being justified by faith, we have peace with God through our Lord Jesus Christ: By whom also we have access by faith into this grace wherein we stand, and rejoice in hope of the glory of God. And not only so, but we glory in tribulations also: knowing that tribulation worketh patience; And patience, experience; and experience, hope: And hope maketh not ashamed; because the love of God is shed abroad in our hearts by the Holy Ghost which is given unto us.

ROMANS 5:1–5

IN THE PRECEDING CHAPTER I ADDRESSED THE TWO MAIN MEDICAL CONCERNS in the hospital, my spine and my digestion. In this chapter I will tell you the story of my stay in the hospital. This chapter will, due to the length of my hospital stay, reveal a lot about my state of mind.

I entered the orthopedic ward on the twentieth of January. Initially, I was still very weak and all my focus was around starting to convalesce. It was in this week that I was attacked heavily by Satan, trying his best to convince me that I was still dying. As soon as I started to listen to the praise and worship music in my room, that anguish subsided.

I had something to look forward to. My thirtieth birthday was on Monday the twenty-seventh. My family planned a little party for me. They invited some friends from Hamilton too. Being a public holiday, everyone made an effort to be there. It was a very special day for me and the first time since the accident that I had that many people visit me at once. It dawned on me that day that all these people thought that they were going to attend my funeral a few weeks earlier and not celebrate my thirtieth birthday. I felt really blessed that day.

I got spoiled with many beautiful presents. Most were grooming products. I started using them straightaway. I really made an effort to take good care of my hair, nails, and skin while in the hospital. My social worker said that I was the only patient she could recall that would put on some mascara and lip gloss in the mornings.

The reason behind this was an attempt to regain some dignity. When you're that gravely ill, you constantly have teams of physicians examining you, seeing parts of you that you usually conceal. You are wearing hospital attire, which means that when you are moved a variety of people can see parts of you that you would rather have no one see.

To a doctor, you are a patient. Their main concern is treating you by any means necessary. How you might feel about all the extra exposure is a nonissue to them. Not because your needs aren't important, but because at that stage it is secondary. One day I got very agitated when the surgeon and his interns were prodding at me. One intern looked at his peers and told them that this woman had lost all her dignity, and that they should be more sensitive to my needs. I was very impressed with his observation. I thought about it for a while and realized that I should make the best of my situation, and that is when I really started focusing on my grooming.

At that point I was still convinced that my hospital stay would only be for another week or two. I was told that I could leave as soon as my intestines were able to digest food. During this time I felt very optimistic. I was excited that I could start with intense physiotherapy as soon as I was released. In my mind this "nightmare" was going to be over by mid-February.

It was sometime during the last week of January that my food started leaking through my fistulas. I got transferred to the surgical ward. It became clear then that I would have to remain in hospital until these fistulas healed. That news was devastating. It was the start of an immense emotional struggle. I knew in my heart that God was in control and that I was a testimony for His love. On the other hand, I desperately missed my husband and children and longed to be with them. I went through periods of intense self-pity.

I am ashamed to confess the following. At that point I was fully aware of all the miracles God performed to keep me alive. I had emotionally and intellectually processed all the awesome deeds God facil-

itated. Yet, my self-pity would not subside. I spent hours trying to figure out why I had to be the one to suffer. Why I had to lie here and not
be able to bond with my baby. Why I had to lose my ability to walk and
digest food. Poor me! The self-pity would then be followed by periods
of guilt. God saved my life! I shouldn't feel sorry for myself. I should
be glad and worship God. Why am I such a terrible person? It was a
vicious cycle of self-pity, followed by guilt, followed by self-pity.

Nico was back at work by now. He usually had Wednesdays off
and would then travel up from Hamilton to see me. After visiting me,
he would then travel a further 40 km. north to where my brothers lived
to see the children.

The children lived in Auckland during my hospital stay. It was
decided that we would split the two children. My daughter lived with
my eldest brother, Kenny, and his family. Their house was directly
opposite a daycare facility, and as everyone worked full time, Trinita
would have to go there. My mother and Christian stayed with my other
brother John. My mother got permission from the government to stay
on for another ten months. Having the person who raised me now raise
my little ones was an incredible blessing to me.

My mother would visit me three to four times a week. Initially, it
wasn't such a difficult undertaking because my dad was still here and
he could assist her. As soon as he returned to South Africa, though, my
mother's frequent visits with a small baby became a major source of
stress for her. She had to travel from the northern suburbs of Auckland
to its southern districts. It was an approximate distance of 40 km. What
made the journey all the more challenging was extensive road construction and its consequent traffic jams. My mother would often arrive
at the hospital completely flushed and fatigued.

It was really difficult for me to see her that way. I knew it could not
have been easy for a sixty-five-year-old woman to cart around a baby
and all his gear. I was also very apprehensive about them travelling that
far. For quite a while after the accident, the thought of road travel
instilled a certain amount of fear in my heart. I witnessed firsthand

how ruthless motorcar accidents could be. The thought of my loved ones going about their daily lives on the highways of Auckland terrified me. Knowing what I'd gone through, my biggest fear in those days was having someone I love meet a similar fate.

I knew the time my mother would arrive. I then calculated the amount of time it would take her to travel form the North Shore, and then spent that time praying for their safe arrival.

Seeing my little boy brought me so much joy, knowing that he would leave in an hour gave me so much sorrow. The thing that I found the most frustrating, though, was not being able to be his mummy. I was too weak to really respond to his needs. So, even with me around, he needed someone else to feed, burp, and clean him. I soon started to feel more and more detached from him. It didn't feel like he was mine. That also contributed hugely to my pity parties.

Trinita would come and see me on Saturdays. When you see someone every day you don't realize how much they grow physically and mature mentally. Seeing her once a week was an eye-opener. Every time I saw her she was bigger than before, and she could communicate more readily. I always got the sense from her that she was trying to be "tough" for me. She seemed confident and on top of things. She confessed to me months later that she had cried herself to sleep every night.

Trinita and I had always been close. When we moved to New Zealand, there were basically just the two of us. Nico worked long hours and his job took him away often. Trinita became the only constant source of comfort in my life. Seeing her only once a week was by far the most heart-wrenching experience in the hospital. I needed her so badly.

To add to all the above-mentioned issues, I had a lot to come to terms with. I never really gave the fact that I had an ileostomy bag much thought until then. An ileostomy bag is a bag that is pasted onto your abdomen, over an exposed part of your small intestine. So much of my digestive tract was severed that the only way I could get rid of my bodily waste was through this bag. When I looked down, I saw four holes in my abdomen, oozing with puss, and a strange-looking bag. It was a great source of despair. The thought of me doing my number twos into a bag repulsed me. I just couldn't seem to come to terms with it.

After being in the surgical ward in a single room for about two weeks, I was moved to a double room. The charge nurse, Chantelle, thought it would be wise to pair me up with someone. My roommate was called Glenda. We were about the same age. We were both mothers to young children. Both of us underwent unimaginable trauma to our young bodies. We bonded immediately and spent the days chatting away. Unfortunately, it didn't last. Glenda was diagnosed with Methicillin-resistant staphylococcus aureus (MRSA), a bacterial infection that could be potentially fatal in hospital. It was imperative that she be moved into isolation. We still communicated via notes past on by nurses, and when Glenda went home weeks later, she came to visit me in the hospital and in the spinal unit.

Three days after Glenda went into isolation, I was also diagnosed with MRSA. At that point I thought that the only disadvantage would be isolation. The nurse then explained to me that the presence of the bacteria would retard the healing process of the fistulas. It was a serious blow to my state of mind. I felt utterly hopeless. I found myself crying constantly, not making sense of any of this. I really started to believe that I was being punished.

I called out to God for answers. I didn't get any answers, only a request. *Be patient.* That was absolutely, unequivocally the last thing I wanted to be. Patient! Yet it was the only thing God required of me at that time.

He was faithful during those dark days in the hospital. He blessed me with three more miracles.

All three of the following miracles are about the presence of the right person at the right place at the right time. Many of the miracles mentioned previously have also been like that. There are the sceptics out there that would not classify these as miracles. They would dismiss them as coincidences or duty. Ponder this for minute: There are currently approximately 6.6 billion people on this planet. In a city like Auckland, there is a population of 1 million. At what stage would you relinquish your view in favor of the notion that certain people's presence in your life is a direct consequence of God's mighty plan for you?

MIRACLE NO. 11

The Orderly

Graham was an orderly who felt immense empathy for me. He was a theater orderly and saw me during my numerous surgeries. His twelve-hour shifts started at noon. Being a devout Christian himself, he took it upon himself to visit me every evening at 9.30 during his break and pray for me. After the prayer he would tuck me in and turn the lights off. He was a gentle and soft spoken man, and his presence was greatly appreciated.

What made Graham so special was not only his act of friendship toward me, but his physical appearance too. Graham resembled my father. When I looked at Graham, I could see my daddy. Of all the Christian orderlies in the entire world, God guided me to the one who looked like my own daddy. God thinks of everything. Halleluiah!

MIRACLE NO. 12

The Social Worker

Every hospital ward is assigned a social worker. Their duty is to try to see to the emotional needs of the patients. Especially patients like me, who are expected to stay in the hospital for long periods. The social worker for Ward 20, the surgical ward, was called Kerry. Kerry came to see me every weekday. She was an exotically beautiful woman with an intoxicating smile. Two things made Kerry special.

She was a Christian. We immediately had something in common. In today's world, it is not politically correct to advertise your faith. *Medical personnel and social workers can get into trouble if they wear their faith on their sleeve. I learned early on that it was my responsibility to tell anyone caring for me of my faith. If it was established that I was a Christian, the personnel could talk to me openly about Jesus. Kerry's visits were very inspirational. We would pray together and share our experiences in faith. Her daily visits were something I really looked forward to.*

The other thing that made her presence special to me was the personal experience she had with spinal injuries. A year earlier, her twenty-year-old daughter, Anna, fell off a balcony and broke her spine. Kerry was able to give my mother and me some insight to what was to be expected over the next twelve months.

MIRACLE NO. 13

The New Friend

A friend in need is a friend indeed! That phrase will remain a cliché to you until you experience a friendship born in hardship and nurtured with Christ's love.

One Tuesday afternoon I heard a knock at my room door. A lady and two small boys were standing there. Certain that they were at the wrong room, I attempted to direct them back. Just then the lady called out my name. She introduced herself as Sandra Bruin and also pointed to her two sons, Marius and Bernard. I greeted them and she entered my room.

Sandra had only been in New Zealand less than two weeks when my accident occurred. Her minister, Stephan Joubert, mentioned me in a sermon and then suggested to her that she visit me. She made a commitment to herself to visit me twice a week. She would come on a Tuesday afternoon with her two boys, and then on a Friday evening with her husband Titus and the two boys.

We soon became close friends. She is a very warm and loving woman. I soon became dependant on seeing her brighten up my room.

I knew from the beginning that Sandra was from a town called
Papakura. Not being an Auckland native, I did not really know
where Papakura was in relation to the hospital. It was only after
my release that I realized her selflessness. Papakura was quite a
distance from Middlemore hospital. Not only did she attempt
Auckland's ruthless traffic twice a week, but she made the financial
decision to visit me in a time where her family's financial resources
were very limited.

Sandra, Kerry, and Graham reminded me of a story I once heard. There was a salesmen convention in a faraway city. A group of salesmen had to fly out to their intended destination. The final keynote speaker went over his allocated time, making the salesmen potentially late for their flights back home. When they reached the airport, the group of men rushed out of their cabs toward the departure lounge. En route to the departure desk, their path got obstructed by a cart of apples. In their haste, they ran into the cart. The apples got strewn all over the terminal floor. When they reached their gate, one of the salesmen felt that he couldn't leave knowing that he helped overturn the cart. He asked his colleagues to tell his wife that he would be on a later flight and he returned to the overturned cart. As he approached the cart, he saw a young blind girl sitting next to the apples, haplessly trying to salvage her losses. She had tears running down her face. In his heart he immediately knew he did the right thing by returning to her. He knelt down and politely offered her help with restoring her cart. He picked up all the apples. The ones that seemed unharmed he arranged back onto the cart. The damaged apples were collected into a plastic bag and counted. He then reimbursed her for the loss of sales she had. When he was done, he knelt down next to her and tried to console her. Suddenly she stopped crying and asked him, "Sir, are you Jesus?"

I think having that question asked of you is by far the most flattering compliment anyone could ever give you. Sandra, Kerry, and Graham were "Jesus" to me in hospital.

FOOD FOR THOUGHT

There is always a purpose in everything. Even when everything seems to be going wrong, the purpose of it is still in motion. Retrospect is a valuable spiritual tool, never underestimate its importance.

God loves us and never wants us to suffer. Sometimes, however, He can't take the suffering away immediately, and we need to be patient in faith.

God knows every person on this planet, and he knows exactly who to send on your path. Value your acquaintances, family, and friends. They're not there coincidentally!

SOUL SEARCHING

Have you ever felt that God has forsaken you? What were the circumstances surrounding that assumption? Do you honestly believe in your heart that He did indeed forsake you, or did His plan reveal itself in due time?

If you are currently struggling with the issue of God's abandonment, how could you change your thought processes to allow the truth of God's Word and the infallibility of God's love to help you?

James 1: 3–4 says, "My brethren, count it all joy when ye fall into divers temptations; Knowing this, that the trying of your faith worketh patience. But let patience have her perfect work, that ye may be perfect and entire, wanting nothing." In other translations "temptations" are referred to as "testing" or "trials." Do you believe that you need to rejoice when you face faith-building hardships? Have you ever had such an experience? What did God teach you?

James 1:5: "If any of you lack wisdom, let him ask of God, that giveth to all men liberally, and upbraideth not; and it shall be given him." My interpretation of verse 5 is that temptations, trials, or testing are aimed at gaining wisdom. How do you view the passage James 1:3–5?

CHAPTER SEVEN

For we know that the whole creation groaneth and travaileth in pain together until now. And not only they, but ourselves also, which have the firstfruits of the Spirit, even we ourselves groan within ourselves, waiting for the adoption, to wit, the redemption of our body. For we are saved by hope: but hope that is seen is not hope: for what a man seeth, why doth he yet hope for? But if we hope for that we see not, then do we with patience wait for it. Likewise the Spirit also helpeth our infirmities: for we know not what we should pray for as we ought: but the Spirit itself maketh intercession for us with groanings which cannot be uttered. And he that searcheth the hearts knoweth what is the mind of the Spirit, because he maketh intercession for the saints according to the will of God. And we know that all things work together for good to them that love God, to them who are the called according to his purpose.

ROMANS 8:22–28

For whatsoever things were written aforetime were written for our learning, that we through patience and comfort of the scriptures might have hope.

ROMANS 15:4

Wherefore I also, after I heard of your faith in the Lord Jesus, and love unto all the saints, Cease not to give thanks for you, making mention of you in my prayers; That the God of our Lord Jesus Christ, the Father of glory, may give unto you the spirit of wisdom and revelation in the knowledge of him: The eyes of your understanding being enlightened; that ye may know what is the hope of his calling, and what the riches of the glory of his inheritance in the saints, And what is the exceeding greatness of his power to us-ward who believe, according to the working of his mighty power.

EPHESIANS 1:15–19

HOPE

IT WAS NOW TIME FOR ME TO LEAVE MIDDLEMORE HOSPITAL. I WAS discharged at the end of March. I had spent twelve weeks at the hospital, but it felt more like a lifetime. That is why I really dreaded the next part of my journey. I needed to go to a spinal unit to kick-start my rehabilitation. For weeks I tried to somehow get out of it as I was desperate to just get home to my family, but to no avail. There was just no way around it; I absolutely had to spend two weeks at the Otara spinal unit.

On the eve of my discharge, the nurses organized a little farewell party for me, complete with coffee and cake. It just reinforced to me how fortunate I was to be taken care of by such a group of phenomenal caregivers. When I had entered the wards, I was just another patient; by the time I left, I was a friend. I was treated with so much love, compassion, and respect by the nursing staff. It was truly a privilege for me to have met all of them.

The next morning when my orderly arrived to take me to the spinal unit, it was time to greet the day shift nurses. Before we could help ourselves, we had tears pouring down our faces. It was very poignant. The past twelve weeks had been the most painful and dreadful weeks of my life, and yet God still managed to get love and dearness out of the situation.

I was now on my way to Otara. The orderly pushed my wheelchair into the ambulance, and I immediately found myself in an immense predicament. The ambulance only had lap seat belts. There was no other means of restraint. I started trembling and my heart rate soared.

My first reaction was that this was some kind of cruel joke. I felt angry. This was my first car ride since my accident and I was expected to have the object that cut me in half in the first place placed around my waist! Just then God spoke to my heart. What he said was quite remarkable: Ana, you have two choices. You could avoid lap seatbelts for years and build up feelings of fear, resentment, and anxiety around wearing this form restraint, or you can deal with that issue right here, right now. With that sentiment, I clicked my belt and faced my fears. And as always, God was right! I still avoid using the lap seat belt and I forbid my children to sit on a seat restrained that way, but I don't harbor any negative or destructive feelings around the issue. I guess one could say that I "forgave" the lap seat belt that day.

The trip to Otara was short, but for someone stuck in a small room for three months, it was a most enjoyable one. It was a beautiful sunny day, and when I felt the sun on my cheeks, it was like a rush of adrenaline pumping through me, reinforcing that I was still alive.

It took a couple of hours to get settled into my room. I was assessed by the doctors and given my roster for the next two weeks. I was still in isolation as the doctors couldn't risk me infecting any of the other patients with MRSA, so my physiotherapy and occupational therapy sessions were scheduled around the other patients. I was also instructed that I was to have meals in my room and not the dining hall. I was assigned a separate bathroom. All this was intended to prevent contamination, but it made me feel very secluded. I had been in isolation for so long that I desperately craved human contact and interaction.

My first physiotherapy session was the next morning. The physiotherapy was done in a huge gym adjacent to the living quarters. In the gym there was an indoor basketball field and that was flanked by a variety of exercise equipment.

I was really excited to get going. When I saw the various weight machines I couldn't wait to get on it and try it out. I was, however, a bit premature in my expectations of my physical capabilities. Initially, the only way I could attend my physiotherapy sessions was with my wheelchair. Maree, my physiotherapist, gave me an outline of her expectations for the next two weeks. She also gave me an indication of what I should be able to do after the two weeks. The first area of business for her, though, was to teach me how to "fall" and then get up after the fall. We spent two sessions doing various activities of that nature. Still quite naïve about my inability to move readily, I found myself quite impatient. I wanted to start using the leg machines!

After learning the different fall techniques, getting into and out of a car was my next lesson. It was only after four sessions that we got down to the business of exercise and training. By the end of my first week at the spinal unit, I could walk to the gym with my walking frame. It was still a very slow and painful walk, but that didn't deter me. I was making progress! If my physiotherapy session was to start at 10:00, I had to leave my room at 9:45 just to make it in time. I only had about forty five meters to walk, and I used to get to the gym right on time.

Another part of the treatment program was occupational therapy. I had to learn how to do certain household tasks with my current limited capabilities. Between the physiotherapy and occupational therapy, I was kept quite busy. That was a good thing, because it helped pass the time. My excitement at the prospect of going home the next week was almost overwhelming. I so looked forward to reading my little girl a bedtime story and feeding my baby boy a bottle. I even looked forward to changing a poopy nappy. I longed to lie next to my husband at night. I longed to be a family again!

Something else I was excited about was to be able to eat again. I had been on TPN for so long, I had a renewed appreciation for the taste and texture of food. In addition to the hospital meals, my mum brought me some treats. I was like a little child on Christmas Eve. I couldn't eat a lot of food as my stomach had shrunk after months of inactivity, but when I ate, I savored every bite.

One night when the nurse cleaned my wounds, she noticed some unidentifiable leakage from three of the fistulas. I looked down and to my horror saw that my much-enjoyed food was once again seeping up through my intestines. I was understandably upset and the nurse was understandably very concerned. She phoned the hospital and was instructed to send me back to Middlemore to be examined further.

MIRACLE NO. 14

In the preceding twelve weeks, I had the opportunity to thank most of the people who were instrumental in my survival. I spoke to

Lorraine, the nurse at the scene of the accident; I also personally thanked Meesha and Wayne, the two people who took care of my children at the scene. I sent out thank you notes to all families and groups I knew prayed for me. There was one person, though, that I couldn't thank yet: the exceptionally compassionate paramedic. I prayed and asked God to help me get his contact details in order for me to thank him.

The paramedics arrived at the spinal unit to take me back to Middlemore hospital. There were three men. I was transferred from my bed to the gurney and pushed into the back of the ambulance. I was so upset and tearful that I never once looked at any of them. Then one of the men looked intently at me and excitedly exclaimed: "Are you still alive?" Confused, I looked up and saw the face I had imprinted in my mind. This time, though, he did not have a look of concern, but one of astonishment. He then told his colleagues about my accident and my injuries, and excitedly exclaimed that he thought that I was not going to survive. His excitement was so real, it was almost tangible. I realized then that this trip to the hospital was not a setback, but only a carefully orchestrated plan of God to answer my prayer. And it was! Within hours I was back at the spinal unit, ready to continue with my rehabilitation.

Learning to fall and get into a car was not the only thing I learned at the spinal unit. Although I was isolated from the rest of the patients, the utter hopelessness in the facility did not go unnoticed by me. By the second week I could feel my mood dropping. My rehabilitation was going very well and I personally didn't have a reason to feel depressed, but the dark mood surrounding me started to work on my emotions. I was surrounded by para- and quadriplegics who had given up on life. The few people I interacted with were so defeated and depressed. I just did not know how to deal with it. I almost felt guilty for having my hope, for knowing that I would walk again.

The hopelessness I experienced at the spinal unit made it very difficult for me to write about. Quite some time has passed between the conclusion of chapter six and the writing of this chapter. I was at a loss about how I could get a lesson out of that dark aspect of my two weeks there. Then something happened: my expensive pair of sunglasses broke.

They broke during a weekend visit to friends. I had to replace them as I couldn't drive the two-hour trip back home without some protection for my eyes. Being on a budget, I could not replace the branded glasses, so I went to an inexpensive store to find a replacement. These knockoff glasses were pretty funky and I looked quite good in them. Car trunk packed and glasses on, we drove back home.

It was April and autumn in New Zealand. New Zealand is a breath-taking country, but I particularly love it in autumn. The coloration of the leaves in New Zealand is really something to experience. There are shades of every brown, every copper, every red, and every yellow imag-inable. I would go for drives in the country this time of year just to take photographs of this beautiful natural phenomena.

This year was different. It seemed like autumn on steroids. The leaves were more radiant and splendid than ever. Added to its remark-able color were glints of sparkle. Over the next two months I marvelled in the beauty of this particular autumn. Every day during my carpool I would look down into a tree-lined valley on the way to the children's school and feel a renewed sense of appreciation for Mother Nature. One sunny afternoon I was running late and rushed out of the house without my funky shades. It was a very sunny day and as always I gazed down at the valley to admire the Technicolor view. That day, though, it all seemed rather ordinary. It looked like any other autumn day. I attributed it to the angle of the sun.

The next day, with my sunglasses on, I did the same trip. This time the valley was luminescent again. Suspicious, I lifted my glasses to dis-cover, with disappointment, that it was yet another ordinary autumn day. I finally realized that the sunglasses were responsible for my renewed appreciation of this time of year. Right then God spoke to my heart and told me to liken the cheap sunglasses to hope. When you have God in your life, it's like wearing a cheap pair of sunglasses. Everything seems more beautiful, more radiant, and more meaningful. There is something I had in the spinal unit that the few people I met did not have: hope. And hope, like grace and mercy, is a gift directly from God.

FOOD FOR THOUGHT

God works in mysterious ways. He orchestrated a reason for me to need a paramedic. Romans 5:2–3 states, "By whom also we have access by faith into this grace wherein we stand, and rejoice in hope of the glory of God. And not only so, but we glory in tribulations also: knowing that tribulation worketh patience; And patience, experience; and experience, hope." Trials and tribulations are a part of life. Having God in your heart gives you hope during the most trying times.

SOUL SEARCHING

I hated my three months in the hospital. I was at times very angry and resentful for having to spend so much time there. Yet, God gave me something positive to hang on to: the gentleness and dearness of my caregivers. Have you ever been in a situation that you absolutely dreaded, just to have the opportunity of hindsight to see a positive angle?

The last thing I wanted was to sit in a lap seat belt. Have you ever been in a situation where you were forced by God to face your fears/mistakes/poor judgement calls?

God used a cheap pair of sunglasses to teach me a lesson. Think back at a time where God used an every day item to make a point.

CHAPTER EIGHT

For I reckon that the sufferings of this present time are not worthy
to be compared with the glory which shall be revealed in us.

ROMANS 8:18

And our hope of you is stedfast, knowing, that as ye are partakers
of the sufferings, so shall ye be also of the consolation.

2 CORINTHIANS 1:7

I INVADED MY DAUGHTER'S OXFORD DICTIONARY IN THE HOPE OF MAKING this chapter as descriptive and accurate as possible. I thought that I if had a huge list of adjectives and adverbs I could bring home to you how much I suffered the first six months at home. My list started with abysmal and ended with writhe. I was resolute in getting my point across. I suffered!

I was discharged from the spinal unit on the eleventh of April 2003. That day is and will always be imprinted in my mind as the day of my homecoming. A homecoming I naively assumed would be easy. I mean, what could go wrong? I am going home!

The first part of our trip was north. We had to travel from Otara in the south of Auckland to Auckland's North Shore to pick up my mother and the children. My excitement was translucent. I could not wait to be able to tell my little girl that mummy was coming home with her today. I drew a little wall chart for her weeks earlier and instructed her that she should cross out a day every evening and know that she is a day closer to having mummy home. As we turned into the road where her kindergarten was, I suddenly felt anxious. What if she didn't want me as her mummy anymore? I had been gone for three months, and to a three-year-old that is like a lifetime. With this anxiety in my heart, Nico escorted me up the ramp and into the kindergarten lobby. He told one of the teachers who we were and she excitedly got up to get Trinita.

I will never forget her face. She looked directly at me, and I could literally see the disbelief and confusion in her eyes. It took a good few seconds for her to realize that it was indeed her mummy and not her imagination. She cautiously walked over to me and gave me a hug, almost afraid that I may break or perhaps disappear again. It was one of the most momentous experiences of my life.

The caregivers at the kindergarten were absolutely exceptional in their care of Trinita. Three months earlier they got a frightened little girl who was suddenly away from her parents and her home. By the time she left, she ruled the roost. I was told by various people that she enjoyed her time at the kindergarten so much that she refused to leave at night. Maelen, my sister-in-law, would come to get her at four in the afternoon. Trinita would then beg her to stay longer, and Maelen would then go home and leave her there for a little while longer. When my nephew, Brandon, got home, Maelen would send him across the street to get Trinita. She was usually still not ready to go home. At five either my brother, Kenny, or my niece, Elaine, would try to convince her to come home, just to have her say that she would only leave if all the children had gone. So, she routinely only got back to their house between five-thirty and six, content as could be. She loved her teachers. She loved her friends. And I love that about her.

We went to Kenny's house to gather her things. Our next stop was John's place to pick up my mother and Christian. Seeing little Christian was less poignant and more disconcerting. The fear of my inability to mother him spoiled my reunion with him. Every time I looked at him, I was overwhelmed by feelings of inadequacy. I so longed to just hold him in my arms, smell his incredible baby scent, and promise him that I was going to be a mother to him in the way that he deserved. But I could not do that.

Nico and I decided not to drive down to Hamilton that evening, but only the next morning. Although I was eager to get home, we could not take on the Friday afternoon traffic in my fragile state. I was, furthermore, not able to sit for long periods at a time without experiencing tremendous pain. We spent the night at John's house. Hamilton had to wait until the next morning.

As you can well imagine, preparing myself mentally and emotionally to travel on that same fateful road was quite a challenge. I was determined to approach it in the same way as the ambulance–lap seat belt incident. I simply had to do it. It was not done, though, without a copious amount of prayer prior, during, and after the trip.

When we approached the stretch of road where the accident occurred, I was delighted to see that the police lowered the speed limit dramatically. Nico told me that it was done shortly after our accident after a public outcry. Now, not only were more people aware of the dangers of lap seat belts, but the reduced speed limit would also drastically reduce the likelihood of a repeat incident, especially since the police were ruthless in their policing of that stretch of road.

As we drove into Hamilton, I was overwhelmed by being home. I was so hopeful and in excited anticipation of my rehabilitation at Waikato Hospital. I was at that stage able to walk with a frame, but soon I would be able to take my first baby steps!

The first week back home was hectic. The first order of business was to establish a routine for the children and to get them settled into life at home. We had an influx of well-wishers and friends offering help and assistance, and without that our homecoming would have been all the more difficult.

I also needed to meet my Hamilton-based case manager for ACC, the Accident Compensation Corporation. ACC is a government-funded insurance company that deals with all kinds of accidents at home, at work, and on the road. ACC already picked up the bill for the past three months and I was about to find out how incredibly comprehensive their rehabilitation plan would be. Along with my "Lifetime" planner, Rayna, and my case manager, Helen, we assessed my needs for the next six months. The first financial contribution ACC wanted to make was toward my mother and two brothers for taking care of the children. It was then established that I would need a full-time nanny to assist my mother with the care of Trinita and Christian. Appointments for occupational therapy and physiotherapy were set up, and I was given all the equipment needed to make my life at home easier. That included a shower chair, special stools, a walking frame, and a wheelchair.

We also did not have the strain of preparing meals as a friend of ours rallied the ladies of the South African community to provide us with dinner every night.

The first week progressed well and I was carefully optimistic about the weeks to come. Soon it became apparent that my optimism had been dismally premature. I started vomiting profusely. I could not keep any solids or liquids down. Weakened considerably by the excessive vomiting and becoming dehydrated pretty quickly, I had my first trip back to the hospital. Waikato Hospital was put on alert by ACC that I was a priority patient, and I was immediately treated for the dehydration. Once I received adequate fluids, I was released again.

Once back home I would slowly start eating things like dry toast and then gradually move to more substantial food. Within days of eating normally, the whole process would repeat itself and I would find myself sleeping in the emergency room again.

Over the next six months I would routinely be rushed to the emergency room. Initially, it was just for symptoms of dehydration, but soon I needed more than just fluids. I needed Valium intravenous drips too.

My inability to eat weakened me tremendously. It also created a vicious cycle of impeding my physiotherapy. Many physiotherapy sessions had to be cancelled because I was simply too weak. During physiotherapy sessions, the physiotherapist needed to carry a little bucket with her because I would vomit my way through the sessions. I was very fortunate because I had a wonderful physiotherapist whom I coincidently knew before my accident. Her name was Lucy and she had the face and temperament of an angel. She treated my rehabilitation with the utmost dearness and understanding. I really don't know how I could have endured my physiotherapy without her.

My uneducated opinion of the vomiting was that somehow my

"new" digestive tract was rejecting food. With my colon and much of my small intestine gone, I wondered whether the remainder of organs knew how to deal with food. It also seemed like the food that was not vomited got secreted into my ileostomy bag within minutes.

The consistency of the feces in the bag was very watery. That resulted in another awful and regular occurrence. The bag would fill up very quickly and burst at the opening. That was by far the most humiliating and emotionally distressing part of my first months at home.

When the bag burst, Nico and my mother had to carry me to the shower. There, one of them would help me to clean up while the other one cleaned the bed. A new plastic protector would then be put on the bed with fresh sheets and blankets. The soiled bedding would then be washed immediately. All this would usually occur in the early morning hours. Before long, Nico would have to get up for work, tired and emotionally drained. My mother would get up to feed Christian with tears in her eyes. I think the experience of soiling myself repeatedly and enduring the humiliation of others cleaning me up has scarred me for life. No other circumstance in the last five years has disgraced me more. No other physical consequence of the accident has affected me more. Soiling myself has scarred me for life.

I soon became suicidal. I was an invalid. I was a burden. I felt like a blob unable to benefit humanity in any way. Two critical things happened that pushed me to the edge: my roommate at Middlemore, Glenda, committed suicide. She too became overwhelmed by her trauma of the past five months. And Christian cried…

I was in lying in bed one morning. My mother was at the store, and Christian, then five months, was in the care of the ACC-appointed nanny. I had been vomiting for days. I was in constant pain, miserably frail, and incapable of moving from the bed. Christian started crying. He kept on crying and crying. After enduring his plea for five minutes, I desperately wanted to placate him. I lifted myself up, slid to the floor, and crawled to the door. With great difficulty I opened the bedroom door and saw him screaming in his rocker. Already exhausted, I crawled closer just to make a startling discovery. The nanny was sitting right next to him reading a novel. In that moment I experienced levels of hopelessness impossible for me to relate. All I wanted was to care for my infant, and I couldn't. Yet, this person entrusted to do so, didn't. I decided then and there that I was going to crawl to the kitchen to get a knife. I was not planning on slitting my wrists. I wanted to pierce the knife into my heart.

MIRACLE NO. 15

To get to the kitchen, I had to crawl past the lounge. It was only approximately five to six meters, but I was already exhausted. I decided to take a breather. I got onto the couch and God spoke to my heart. He asked me to switch on the television and go to Channel 111, the Christian Network. I started watching a program about soldiers in Iraq. Nothing about the program related to my experience, but it gave me hope, and I decided to wait another twenty-four hours before piercing my heart.

During the next few weeks, God taught me a valuable life lesson. Every day I wanted to kill myself and every day he gave me an incentive to carry on for another twenty-four hours. I learned that feelings of depression are inevitable. How you deal with it determines how soon you get on top of it. A conscious decision has to be made every morning that you will get through the day no matter what. Most mornings that decision was very difficult to make, yet it had to be made. God taught me that happiness is a choice.

After the incident with the nanny, my mother started praying for a suitable replacement and that's how miracle number sixteen came into our lives.

MIRACLE NO. 16

Her name was Clare. Clare means light and that is what she brought to us. Clare was in her early twenties, full of life, and in love with children. Her care of Christian was second to none. She managed to give him ample love and attention. For the next eighteen months, Clare was a part of our household.

My physical state did not improve; in fact, it worsened. My emotional state also deteriorated at an alarming rate. Over a period of a month I became more and more aggressive. I would periodically scream at my mother and Nico, most of the time for no apparent reason. I recall one day chasing my mother away. I told her very crudely to go back to South Africa. One evening Nico made me some herbal tea. He put in one spoon of sugar instead of two. I got so angry that I wanted to use my "suicide knife" to stab him. I was not myself, but I was not in a position to know that.

My aggressive demeanor also alienated some friends. There was one occasion where a friend phoned and asked me how I was doing. I ended up screaming at her. She never phoned me ever again. In fact, she avoided me like the plaque after that.

I wish I could say that it only happened with that one friend. Quite a few people were spooked by my erratic behavior, resulting in a few friendships fading. I still sometimes wish I could explain that it was not me acting that way. When I feel that way I am reminded of the friends who stuck by me regardless of my aggressive, irrational rampages, and I view myself as lucky. I realize now that my strange behavior served as some kind of sieve. It separated the genuine form the insincere.

We were still in the dark about my inability to keep food down and my strange anxiety attacks, coupled with extreme aggression. My GP felt absolutely hopeless. She referred me to every specialist, had blood taken for every illness, and we still couldn't get to the bottom of it.

Dottie, my GP, sent a nurse specializing in patients with ileostomy bags to my house. The nurse examined me and matter-of-factly asked me about my Loperamide dosage. I was at that time on a wide variety of medication, but Loperamide was not one of it. After she left I immediately went to Dottie and she prescribed me eight two-milligram Loperamide tablets a day, as per the nurse's recommendation. Loperamide is the other name for Imodiom, the diarrhea drug. As it turns out, I must take this drug for the rest of my life. Not having a colon to extract excess fluid from the feces, Loperamide must fill the gap. Within days of taking the Loperamide, the content in my bag thickened and I was considerably less dehydrated. With this issue overcome, we still needed to get to the bottom of my vomiting, anxiety attacks, and aggression. For this, Dottie sent me to an anesthetist for an overhaul of my medication.

What he discovered alarmed him tremendously and revealed to him why I had suffered so much in the preceding months. Three of my medications were very potent drugs, and I had been given the wrong dosages. In effect, all my "anxiety" attacks were not anxiety attacks at all, but withdrawal symptoms and side effects due to the wrongly prescribed dosages of one drug in particular.

It was such a relief to learn that my vomiting, excessive shaking, and strange behavior would soon be something of the past. Ironically, had I had a history with illicit drug abuse, I would have known sooner that I was experiencing withdrawal.

The anesthetist and I retraced my steps to pinpoint where I was given this wrong information. We found that it was a doctor at the spinal unit that wrote the prescriptions. I don't view that doctor as incompetent, just a bit inexperienced. He was not my lead physician, but the only one on duty on the day of my discharge. My case was much more complex and comprehensive than the average patient he would encounter. I truly think that he was not familiar with the cocktail of medications I was on. He was also not aware of my need for Loperamide. His most crucial mistake was to instruct me to stop my consumption of twelve Gabapentyn capsules a day and to take that medication only when experiencing pain.

I have since excessively researched the various drugs I was on and I will now endeavour to describe in layman's terms what I believed went wrong in my body.

Gabapentin (brand name Neurontin) is a medication originally developed for the treatment of epilepsy. Gabapentin is widely used to relieve pain, especially neuropathic pain. Gabapentin side effects that I suffered included drowsiness, weakness, dizziness, headaches, shaking of my body that I could not control, anxiety, nausea, and vomiting. Withdrawal symptoms I experienced included nausea, vomiting, and dizziness.

Fentanyl is a powerful opioid analgesic with a potency approximately 81 times that of morphine. I was prescribed the patch. This patch had to be replaced every three days. If for some reason I did not have it ready to replace, I suffered serious withdrawal that included anxiety, rapid heartbeat, fever, chills, sweating, nausea or vomiting, nervousness, irritability, shivering or trembling, and weakness.

Nortriptyline is an antidepressant. What this drug did was make me very sleepy, especially in the mornings. I just could not get out of bed. I learned through my research that I also experienced side effects from this drug. This included dizziness, drowsiness, dryness of mouth, headache, increased appetite (mainly for sweets), nausea, tiredness, diarrhea, and weight gain. It was a mystery to me that someone hardly able to keep food down was gaining weight at such an alarming rate. The anesthetist started weaning me off all three medications. Once I had them out of my system I was literally like a new person. The vomiting stopped almost overnight. My weight gain stabilized. The anxiety and mood swings disappeared. I had no more palpitations. I regained my strength at a very encouraging rate. It was October. With ten months of misery behind me, I started to gain a clearer perspective of my situation. I became more positive and any thoughts of suicide disappeared. I then started toying with the idea of writing a book about my experiences...

FOOD FOR THOUGHT

Trials and tests are inevitable. God will bring hardships on your way to test your commitment to Him and to make you stronger. How you choose to deal with hardships will greatly affect the way you grow from them. You can choose to be happy in the midst of hardships. You can also choose to humbly endure hardships in the knowledge that God is in charge. You are human, you may become depressed, but you can choose whether you want to remain depressed or not.

SOUL SEARCHING

Recall a time in your life that you felt was unbearably difficult:

- How did you get through that time?
- What did God teach you from that hardship?
- Could you see God in the midst of that hardship?

Chapter Nine

"Our Father which art in heaven, Hallowed be thy name. Thy kingdom come. Thy will be done in earth, as it is in heaven. Give us this day our daily bread. And forgive us our debts, as we forgive our debtors. And lead us not into temptation, but deliver us from evil: For thine is the kingdom, and the power, and the glory, for ever. Amen.

For if ye forgive men their trespasses, your heavenly Father will also forgive you:

But if ye forgive not men their trespasses, neither will your Father forgive your trespasses."

Matthew 6:10–15

FORGIVENESS

THIS IS THE STORY OF HOW I CAME TO FORGIVE THE MAN WHO CAUSED THE accident. As with most criminal activities, there were conflicting stories about the events of the fifth of January 2003—the view of the police and the statement of the man.

The death of the man's partner at the scene of the accident brought criminal charges against him. He now potentially faced lengthy jail time for the fatality.

The police were of the opinion that the man was intoxicated—a view supported by the time of day and year, as well as incriminating evidence found at the accident scene. The accident occurred in broad daylight, bringing the notion of him falling asleep at the wheel into question. Furthermore, it was during a very festive time of year when police are bombarded with drunk-driving offenses. The most incriminating thing, though, was the various bottles of alcohol at the footrests of the backseat of his car.

The police were unable to test the man's blood alcohol levels and were thus not able to prove their suspicions. I don't know why his blood alcohol levels were not tested, but I presume it was because of his fragile state and enormous blood loss.

If he had indeed been intoxicated, he would be guilty of manslaughter in the death of his partner and attempted murder for my injuries.

The man, in his early sixties, always contended that he had blacked out. At his trial there were neurologists to confirm this and he was thus found not guilty.

Four months after the accident, I got a phone call from this man emphatically apologizing for the accident. When I put the phone down and reflected on my conversation, I realized that I harbored no ill feeling toward him. I had already forgiven him months ago!

The life lesson that led to this unconditional forgiveness happened twelve years prior to the accident. I must now take you on a journey across the world to Johannesburg, South Africa, in pre-Mandela times.

You first need to have a glimpse of the circumstances I grew up in. I am the daughter of a Portuguese immigrant father and an Afrikaner mother. I grew up in the infamous time of the South African apartheid era where a segregation policy had turned into brutal racism. I lived a paradox. At my Afrikaans school I was surrounded by students whose parents were conservative right wing advocates. At home I had parents who taught me to love and respect all people regardless of their race. My father always put his money where his mouth was, and I constantly witnessed his generosity and kindness toward a people who were then viewed as "inferior."

Those were volatile times. Clashes between the National Party Government and the African National Congress "terrorists" were the order of the day. When I was eight years old, my family and I were in a building adjacent to one that got bombed. I can recall at least three occasions where all the shoppers of our local mall had to be evacuated because of bomb threats. All public facilities had metal detectors and armed guards on the lookout. There were curfews in place for black people. People of color were not allowed to share our toilets, restaurants, entertainment facilities, schools, and even, tragically, our churches.

To the rest of the world, the white South African was the epitome of evil—something I found hard to comprehend. I was very young and very naïve. Also, I didn't know any better. When you grow up in a system of government that spans decades, you are inclined to think that it's the way things are supposed to be.

In early 1990, the then-president, F. W. de Klerk, announced the release of a prisoner called Nelson Mandela. The whole world was abuzz with the news and I was pretty dumbfounded by all the hype. Frankly, I didn't even know who this man was. I was seventeen and at the beginning of my final school year. I had more "important" things to worry about—like designing my prom dress and deciding on a hairdo! You know—important stuff!

Little did I know that the release of this prisoner was the first in a series of events that matured my view of the commandment: "Thou shalt love thy neighbour as thyself."

On the eighth of September 1990, tragedy struck our family. My one brother, Archie, was gunned down in an ambush. His car was hijacked and his wallet taken. He managed to survive for three days before passing away. All this occurred in the neighboring country of Mozambique. That country was in the midst of civil war, and the details of the attack were always a bit sketchy. Eyewitness accounts indicated that there was more than one attacker and that they were armed with AK-47 automatic rifles. The one eyewitness remarked on how young the attackers were, and it is thought that they were child soldiers between the ages of twelve and fifteen.

Archie's death hit me particularly hard. I had five brothers and I loved them all dearly, but Archie always made me feel like a princess. He always had flattering things to say to me, and being an awkward and insecure teenager, I fed on his compliments. His death also happened a few days before the commencement of my second last series of final examinations. I had a complete mental breakdown, knowing that I was not able to give all my attention to my studies. I realize now that my perfectionism caused it. I just could not face having less than A's and my fragile mourning state would ensure that.

It was the first time in my life that I lost someone close to me and thus the first time I had to deal with the different phases of mourning. When I got to the "anger" phase, I suddenly found myself enraged at the perpetrator. I started harboring feelings of racism and hatred completely uncharacteristic of my nature. I was now eighteen and eligible to vote, and for the first time in my life my views on apartheid actually mattered. And for the first time in my life I supported it unequivocally. I was so consumed with hatred toward the murderer, all I could see was his color. He was black! So, he had to be evil!

The anger and hatred started overwhelming me. I would find myself plotting ways to get back at "them." Consumed with anger and pain and unable to write my exams, I became increasingly depressed. Although I was very young, I already knew that God and God alone could help me through my depression. When I felt particularly low, I would go to the lounge and play some gospel music. After which I would have some quiet reflective time, followed by trying to "listen" to God. On one such day God asked me something. He asked: "Other than the murderer being black, what else do you know about him?" Well, I knew that he was between twelve and fifteen years old. I immediately thought of Josh McDowell.

Josh McDowell is an American preacher. I frequently watched his sermons on television. I had also read a book he cowrote with Dick Day called Why Wait: What You Need to Know about the Teen Sexuality Crisis. McDowell usually preached around one theme: When children feel unconditional love from their parents, they are less likely to be promiscuous. He would often say that it was more important for parents to love one another than it was for them to love their children. All this was done around the topic of teenage sexual abstinence. God wanted me to apply the biblical truths I'd learnt from Josh McDowell to the murder of my brother.

I spent weeks mulling everything around my head. What could his teachings possibly have in common with a hateful and murderous guerrilla terrorist? Then one night, out of the blue, I had a "God moment." You know…an epiphany brought about by reading a piece of Scripture you had read a thousand times before.

God told me that the key was love. He showed me that the person who pulled the trigger was not a man, but a boy. He reminded me that Josh McDowell always preached the importance of parental love. Then He asked me: "What makes a twelve-year-old capable of cold-blooded murder?" The answer: Not knowing what love is.

I don't know who pulled the trigger. For all I know he was orphaned, or worse, viciously taken from his parents to serve in the army. I realized that I had no right to hate him.

Feeling ashamed and filled with sorrow, I begged God to show me what to do. All He said was: "Love him."

I then prayed and asked God to let the boy know that I forgive him and that I love him. He would never meet me, but I knew by consciously feeling love toward him, God would somehow make him aware that somewhere out there someone cares.

The next morning I awoke with no feelings of animosity. My hatred was gone. My irrational support of extreme racial segregation had disappeared. In its place, color blindness. God taught me that love transcends age, race, color, and most importantly, in this case, tragedy.

(I am still occasionally guilty of racial thoughts and will sometimes laugh at racial jokes. I always feel tremendous guilt and shame after it, because the lesson of unconditional love toward all was a lesson taught to me by God himself.)

I only realized in 2003, twelve years after God taught me that important life lesson, how profound it all hit home. I was truly and unequivocally able to forgive the man who caused the accident. That made me realize an important truth about God. If he uses major events in your life to teach you His way, he imprints those lessons so deeply inside your heart that it is impossible for you to forget them.

FOOD FOR THOUGHT

If God wants to teach you a life truth, He will ensure that you never forget it. He will imprint it deep into your heart.

"Love thy neighbor" means everybody, not just the few people you deem "important" enough to be your neighbor.

SOUL SEARCHING

Can you recall a time when you sensed that God was trying to teach you a lesson? What was it? How have you consequently applied the principle in your life?

What was society teaching you about people who are different to you when you were growing up? How has that view changed in adulthood? How can you wholeheartedly accept to truth that all people are equally as important and equally loved by God?

CHAPTER TEN

And the Word was made flesh, and dwelt among us, (and we beheld his glory, the glory as of the only begotten of the Father,) full of grace and truth.

JOHN 1:14

But we believe that through the grace of the Lord Jesus Christ we shall be saved, even as they.

ACTS 15:11

Therefore by the deeds of the law there shall no flesh be justified in his sight: for by the law is the knowledge of sin. But now the righteousness of God without the law is manifested, being witnessed by the law and the prophets; Even the righteousness of God which is by faith of Jesus Christ unto all and upon all them that believe: for there is no difference: For all have sinned, and come short of the glory of God; Being justified freely by his grace through the redemption that is in Christ Jesus: Whom God hath set forth to be a propitiation through faith in his blood, to declare his righteousness for the remission of sins that are past, through the forbearance of God;

To declare, I say, at this time his righteousness: that he might be just, and the justifier of him which believeth in Jesus. Where is boasting then? It is excluded. By what law? of works? Nay: but by the law of faith. Therefore we conclude that a man is justified by faith without the deeds of the law. Is he the God of the Jews only? is he not also of the Gentiles? Yes, of the Gentiles also: Seeing it is one God, which shall justify the circumcision by faith, and uncircumcision through faith.

ROMANS 3:20–30

Therefore being justified by faith, we have peace with God through our Lord Jesus Christ: By whom also we have access by faith into this grace wherein we stand, and rejoice in hope of the glory of God. And not only so, but we glory in tribulations also: knowing that tribulation worketh patience; And patience, experience; and experience, hope: And hope maketh not ashamed; because the love of God is shed abroad in our hearts by the Holy Ghost which is given unto us.

ROMANS 5:1–5

And he said unto me, My grace is sufficient for thee: for my strength is made perfect in weakness. Most gladly therefore will I rather glory in my infirmities, that the power of Christ may rest upon me.

2 CORINTHIANS 12:9

But this I say, He which soweth sparingly shall reap also sparingly; and he which soweth bountifully shall reap also bountifully. Every man according as he purposeth in his heart, so let him give; not grudgingly, or of necessity: for God loveth a cheerful giver. And God is able to make all grace abound toward you; that ye, always having all sufficiency in all things, may abound to every good work.

2 CORINTHIANS 9:6–8

For by grace are ye saved through faith; and that not of yourselves: it is the gift of God: Not of works, lest any man should boast.

EPHESIANS 2:8–9

Who hath saved us, and called us with an holy calling, not according to our works, but according to his own purpose and grace, which was given us in Christ Jesus before the world began.

2 TIMOTHY 1:9

GRACE

I NEVER GAVE MY NAME MUCH THOUGHT UNTIL I STARTED REFLECTING ON the accident and its influence on my life. Throughout the Bible there are examples of God changing the names of His followers. Abram became Abraham. Saul became Paul. God did not "instruct" me to change my name; I did so voluntarily, in order to glorify His name.

I was christened Ana Marie Doria Trindade. Trindade is Portuguese for *trinity*. Doria is my grandmother's maiden name. It is Portuguese tradition to have two surnames—your father's surname and your grandmother's maiden name. Doria is derived from the Greek word Doris, which means *gift*.

Ana is the Spanish, Portuguese, Slovene, Bulgarian, Romanian, Croatian, Serbian, Macedonian, and Georgian form of the English *Anna*. Both names are derived from the Hebrew word, *Hannah*, which means *favor* or *grace*.

Marie means bitter. It is derived from the Hebrew word *Mara*. When Moses led the Israelites out of Egypt, they came to a place called Marah. Exodus 15:23 says, "And when they came to Marah, they could not drink of the waters of Marah, for they were bitter: therefore the name of it was called Marah."

When reflecting on my life, I realized that "Marie" did not belong in my name anymore. In the "old me," bitter was an accurate description at times. The "new me" is *not* bitter. The "new me" is the result of "grace being a gift from the Trinity" —Ana Doria Trindade.

As you've read my account of the accident and all the following miraculous happenings, you may have thought that I was shown all these wonderful signs because I was a consistent devout follower of Christ. That is not the case. In fact, at the time of the accident, I was probably further away from Christ than I have ever been. *If miracles were given to those who deserve them, they would simply not exist.*

I was raised in a Christian household. My father is Catholic and my mother a Protestant. Although each continued in their own religious beliefs without the one converting to the other, there was one thing they unequivocally agreed on: their children would know God. We had a relatively strange religious upbringing. On Fridays we attended the Protestant church youth group, and on Sundays we attended Mass. We learnt the doctrines of both diverse religions and endured ridicule by those who favored one over the other. Upon reflection, I would not have wanted to grow up under any other circumstances. Too many people put too much emphasis and "faith" into a church doctrine and the human interpretation of the doctrine and not enough emphasis on the truth.

Jesus said unto him, Thou shalt love the Lord thy God with all thy heart, and with all thy soul, and with all thy mind. This is the first and great commandment.

And the second is like unto it, Thou shalt love thy neighbour as thyself.

MATTHEW 22:37–39

AND

For God so loved the world, that he gave his only begotten Son, that whosoever believeth in him should not perish, but have everlasting life.

JOHN 3:16

AND

For I am persuaded, that neither death, nor life, nor angels, nor principalities, nor powers, nor things present, nor things to come, Nor height, nor depth, nor any other creature, shall be able to separate us from the love of God, which is in Christ Jesus our Lord.

ROMANS 8:38–39

As I mentioned earlier, my walk with the Lord started to mature after my brother's murder. Up until then I was still a child in my faith. I believed like a child and nothing had yet come my way to test my beliefs. When Archie died I was confronted with life and death and the completely pointless taking of a young human being. I grew tremendously from that experience, and it prepared me for the next few years of my life.

Unfortunately, my newfound relationship with God did not last long. As a teenager and young adult I struggled with a very low self-esteem. I could not stand the person I saw in the mirror. At sixteen I developed bulimia with the preposterous and misguided notion that I would accept myself if I were ridiculously slim.

Around the time of my brother's death, I was frightfully thin. I concealed it by wearing baggy clothing. My health deteriorated in the following twelve months. I suffered from intense migraine headaches that kept me out of school for weeks on end. My parents were at a loss. I underwent every conceivable test to determine the source of my headaches. It turned out to be hormonal. My drastic weight loss stopped my menstrual cycle, which in turn, put my entire hormonal balance out of sync, and that resulted in excruciating headaches.

My parents knew that I was very fragile emotionally, so they immediately sent me for counselling after Archie's death. The psychiatrist prescribed me with an antidepressant called Emdalen. In the first three months of taking that medication, I inexplicably gained 15kg. I was a teenage girl obsessed with my weight and I equated happiness with a certain number on the scale. That weight gain made my depression worse. I was ashamed to be seen in public. My mum would beg me to go to the mall with her. I felt too ugly to show myself to other people. I was truly a tormented soul.

God tried hard in those times to show me my true value, but I was too blinded by what society deemed attractive. My foolish viewpoint pretty much personified "Ana Marie."

I was taken off the antidepressants after twelve months. The absence of the chemicals in the medication triggered another unpleas-ant experience. As a teenager, I was very fortunate to not get acne. I always had flawless skin. Stopping Emdalen triggered an outbreak of acne on my skin at age nineteen. I am not talking about a few pimples here and there. I am talking about monstrous, throbbing, yellow puss all over my once-pristine complexion! It was not a pretty picture and it only fueled my self-hatred.

It took my body a good two years to recover from the repercussions of the medication. By the end of 1993, my skin was clear and my weight was slowly stabilizing. I had just finished my first year at a uni-versity and I was looking forward to my twenty-first birthday. For the first time in my life I started noticing boys noticing me. I started dat-ing my first boyfriend in May 1994. Having someone in my life who was in love with me helped me alter my view of myself, and slowly but surely I started liking the person I saw in the mirror.

In 1994 my mother also sent me to an organization that helps people "fall in love" with food. It is run by psychologists and its aim is to get people to have a healthy relationship with food and eating. After the completion of the course, I lost all the excess weight I gained from Emdalen. I also realized the importance of physical exercise. My new-found lifestyle resulted in a much happier Ana Marie and also, as a result of the exercise, a much sexier one too.

My boyfriend broke up with me in February 1996. What followed was a year of "sowing my wild oats." Soon after the breakup I was inun-dated with invitations by different men to dinner and movies. The shy, awkward, good little Catholic girl, was replaced by a confident, viva-cious, and utterly shallow babe.

The problem was that the shy, awkward, good little Catholic girl still made time for God. The confident, vivacious, and shallow babe did not want Him to cramp her style. I turned my back on God com-pletely.

Graciously, that period did not last long. In February 1997, I met Nico. Nico brought me back to God. He was very close to God at the time that we met. He started taking me to church again, and he also took me for spiritual counseling to give me an opportunity to have God cleanse me from my "wild" 1996.

We were married in September 1998, committed to a life together with God as navigator. Within six months we were pregnant with Trinita. By the time she turned one we already had all our plans in place for moving to New Zealand.

We arrived in the country in early 2001. Nico got an exceptionally good job and started working straightaway. That is where I moved away from God. It was a perfect opportunity for me to move closer to Him, but I made the wrong decision.

Nico's job took him away from home for weeks on end. I was in a new country, in a strange town. I only had the company of a toddler. I soon became very lonely. I eventually made two friends, but both friendships were short lived. I felt hopelessly isolated.

I know now that if I had reached out to God He would have made the transition from South Africa to New Zealand much smoother for me. I was so determined to adapt to a life in New Zealand without the help of anyone that I foolishly included God in the "anyone" category.

My ego also made an unwelcome comeback in those days. New Zealand is rugby mad. My husband immediately started working in the "inner sanctum" of the ultimate New Zealand passion. I was alone all week. Weekends, though, we mingled with legends and 'celebrities'.

That proved to be a great temptation to the shallow Ana Marie. I became obsessed with my appearance again. I trained six days a week and spent every waking moment consumed with what I would wear and how I would do my hair. I really wanted to fit into this world I was thrust into. I mistakenly believed that I could only do so if I was perfect.

My loneliness started consuming me and I started toying with the idea of having an affair. I know, terrible isn't it? I also started thinking about moving to Auckland to be closer to my brothers.

In April 2002, Nico went abroad for work. He was gone for about a month. I decided that I would go to Auckland and see what it would be like to live there. While I was there I started to feel sick. It took me about a week to realize that it was morning sickness I was experiencing. A home pregnancy test confirmed my suspicions. I was pregnant!

Moving to Auckland was suddenly not an option anymore. I had to go back to Hamilton and my husband.

I had severe morning sickness in the first twelve weeks of the pregnancy. I was miserable. Once again, I had the choice to come closer to God and have Him help me through that difficult time. I opted to instead feel sorry for myself and my awful plight! Once the morning sickness subsided I started enjoying my pregnancy. We found out it was a boy!

I was determined to lose my pregnancy weight as soon as possible. I exercised with gym equipment until three days prior to Christian's birth. Ironically, that obsession played a part in saving my right leg. It is entirely possible that I would have lost my leg had it not been in such a good physical condition.

Once Christian was born, I was resolute in getting back in shape. That was the only thing I could think about, even while in the hospital with double mastitis. I was annoyed at getting the mastitis—not because of it making me so ill, but because my recovery from it would delay my return to exercise and dieting.

I already envisaged what my outfit would look like for my thirtieth and I could already hear the people saying things like, "I can't belief she had a baby only last month! She looks fantastic!" It was all about me! *It was always all about me!* Then the fifth of January 2003 arrived. A day that would define me for all eternity.

So many times in my life when I had a choice and opportunity to be close to God, I turned my back on Him. That day He had the perfect opportunity to turn His back on me. He did not! Instead, He showered me with His grace! He answered the thousands of prayers for my survival and He did so by performing marvelous acts of miraculous intervention. How great is our God?

His grace is one of the many things that make Him so awesome. But what is grace and how do we get it?

I recently watched a documentary on the life of Jeffrey Dahmer. He was an American serial killer who murdered seventeen men and boys, most of whom were of African or Asian descent. His murderous spree started in 1978, with the majority taking place between 1987 and 1991. Mr. Dahmer would lure his victims to his home. He would then rape and torture them until they died. After their death he would again perform sexual acts on the victims. Once the decomposition started, he would dismember them and eventually eat them.

On a scale of one to ten, he would probably score an eleven on a "sinful acts meter." His actions were so morally, socially, and spiritually repugnant that it's hard for most people to view him as a neighbor in the biblical sense.

At the end of the documentary, a pastor was interviewed. This pastor told the interviewer that Dahmer became born-again in prison and accepted Jesus Christ as his personal Lord and Savior. Whether Dahmer was sincere in his repentance is something only he and God would know. For the purposes of this argument, let us assume that Dahmer did wholeheartedly repent and become a Christian.

What does that mean? It means that you and I will share eternity with him in heaven. The self-righteous part of me gets very annoyed at that thought. I don't know about you, but the thought of sharing heaven with someone like him after spending my life trying to live righteously can be a bit disconcerting. Dahmer in heaven, and "Ana Marie" becoming "Ana" is the personification of grace.

Therefore by the deeds of the law there shall no flesh be justified in his sight: for by the law is the knowledge of sin. But now the righteousness of God without the law is manifested, being witnessed by the law and the prophets; Even the righteousness of God which is by faith of Jesus Christ unto all and upon all them that believe: for there is no difference: For all have sinned, and come short of the glory of God; Being justified freely by his grace through the redemption that is in Christ Jesus: Whom God hath set forth to be a propitiation through faith in his blood, to declare his righteousness for the remission of sins that are past, through the forbearance of God;

To declare, I say, at this time his righteousness: that he might be just, and the justifier of him which believeth in Jesus.

ROMANS 3:20–26

Paul is using this passage to teach us about God's abundant grace. Here are his facts on grace:

- Grace is not received through your *deeds*.
- Grace is accepted by *faith*.
- Grace is available to *all* who believe.
- Grace is attained by *justification*.
- Grace is awarded *freely*.
- Grace is acquired through *redemption*.
- Grace is accomplished through *propitiation*.

Most of the above statements are quite self-explanatory. English is my second language, and I will use that excuse when confessing that I did not have a clue what the word propitiation meant. I watched a sermon by the very gifted Dr. David Jeremiah in which he explained it very eloquently: The word appears four times the Bible. When God instructed Moses to build the Ark of the Covenant, one of the instructions included that of a mercy seat.

And thou shalt make a mercy seat of pure gold: two cubits and a half shall be the length thereof, and a cubit and a half the breadth thereof. And thou shalt make two cherubims of gold, of beaten work shalt thou make them, in the two ends of the mercy seat. And make one cherub on the one end, and the other cherub on the other end: even of the mercy seat shall ye make the cherubims on the two ends thereof. And the cherubims shall stretch forth their wings on high, covering the mercy seat with their wings, and their faces shall look one to another; toward the mercy seat shall the faces of the cherubims be. And thou shalt put the mercy seat above upon the ark; and in the ark thou shalt put the testimony that I shall give thee. And there I will meet with thee, and I will commune with thee from above the mercy seat, from between the two cherubims which are upon the ark of the testimony, of all things which I will give thee in commandment unto the children of Israel.

EXODUS 25:17–22

The mercy seat was flanked by two cherubim that looked down on it, and that is where God met His people. Offerings for the sins of the Israelites were made on the mercy seat, covering it in blood. This made it the first way to propitiate (to appease) God for our sins before Jesus became *the* ultimate sacrifice. I also Googled the word and found the following explanation in Wikipedia: "In Christian theology, propitiation is the work of Jesus Christ on the cross, by which he fulfills the wrath of God (both an emotional response of anger and a moral response of indignation), and conciliates him who would otherwise be offended by our sin and would demand that we pay the penalty for it.

"Propitiation is translated from the Greek *hilasterion*, meaning 'that which expiates or propitiates' or 'the gift which procures propitiation.' The word is also used in the New Testament for the place of propitiation, the 'mercy seat.' John mentions propitiation on two occasions: 1 John 2:2: 'And he is the propitiation for our sins: and not for ours only, but also for the sins of the whole world.' Also in 1 John 4:10: 'Herein is love, not that we loved God, but that he loved us, and sent his Son to be the propitiation for our sins.' "

So, grace is accomplished through propitiation. Ergo: without Jesus there is no grace!

Who hath saved us, and called us with an holy calling, not according to our works, but according to his own purpose and grace, which was given us in Christ Jesus before the world began.

2 TIMOTHY 1:9

CHAPTER ELEVEN

"For I say unto you, That except your righteousness shall exceed the righteousness of the scribes and Pharisees, ye shall in no case enter into the kingdom of heaven."

MATTHEW 5:20

SELF-RIGHTEOUSNESS

WHAT IS SELF-RIGHTEOUSNESS? THE DICTIONARY REFERS TO IT AS "PIOUSLY sure of one's own righteousness, being moralistic. Thinking oneself more virtuous than others." Synonyms: holier-than-thou, sanctimonious, pharisaic, and pietistic.

I ashamedly confess that I fell into the Devil's trap of becoming self-righteous. My piety did not stem from all God's good works in my life, but from how people, and in particular, the media, responded to my plight.

The accident made headline news in New Zealand. Not only did the death of the occupant in the other car influence road toll statistics, making it a newsworthy event, but the critical injuries to a young mother—injuries that could have been avoided—also captured the attention of the media.

For a few nights in a row, the national news relentlessly followed the story of the mother in ICU who got "cut in half" by a "legal" form of restraint. The fact that Trinita was only three and, more remarkably, that Christian was only three weeks, made the story all the more poignant. My Intensive Care specialist, Mr. David Gellar, also became very vocal and critical of the lap belt issue. Mr. Gellar felt that he too often had to deal with patients who were restrained in that way, and along with other Intensive Care specialists, called for the government to ban the lap seat belt.

For weeks, journalists closely followed my progress. When it became clear that I not only survived the horrific event, but did so with apparent "superhuman" flair, I was set up for years of media scrutiny.

In the first year after the accident, I was interviewed by various publications on three occasions. Two of the articles were on the front page, accompanied by large photos of me. The third article was for The New Zealand Herald Christmas edition. The newspaper named me the New Zealander who displayed the most courage in 2003. Not only was the article very flattering, but I felt an immense amount of pride. I was in the process of closing the worst year of my life, and my adopted country threw open its arms and said: "We admire you!" It was tremendously encouraging and at the same time very humbling. In that experience, the seed of self-righteousness was planted in my heart.

Where up until then I made every effort to inform people that I was nothing and that my recovery was a product of the grace of God, I started taking some of the credit myself. I believed up until then that God should get all the praise. Suddenly, I felt the little pat I gave myself on the back was not sufficient anymore. I put myself on a pedestal and truly believed, however very fleeting, that that was where I should be. The pride I felt in the way I dealt with the whole situation blinded me.

In 2004 I was approached again. I was first approached in April by the Waikato Times for a follow-up puff piece. In August, the New Zealand Woman's Weekly had an edition that celebrated "Loving the New Zealand Life." In the magazine they chronicled the lives of a few women who had displayed tremendous courage. Every time I was interviewed I could literally sense the curiosity and admiration in the voices of the journalists. That only fueled my ego.

I must admit though, before you want to throw me to the wolves for being so sanctimonious, that I still gave God the credit. I still made sure that they knew that their "story" was the result of multiple miracles. I just enjoyed the attention a little too much.

God, as always, came to the rescue. He spoke to my heart a lot in that time around the subject of my feelings of superiority. He made me feel incredible guilt, which always makes me reflect. He encouraged me not to lose sight of the purpose of it all: to show the world that God performs miracles every day in all sorts of ways.

After the article in the New Zealand Woman's Weekly, I realized that I hadn't exalted God as much as I should have. I was too worried about what the photos were going to look like and whether I was going to look attractive. It was a huge wake-up call for me. I begged God for His forgiveness and asked Him to help me deal with any future attention in an appropriate and Christ-centered way.

Not long after the article appeared on newsstands, I was approached once again—this time by Pietra Brettkelly, a director for Top Shelf Productions. The productions company was making a series called "The Survivor Files" and was interested in featuring my story as one episode. They started shooting in November 2004. All the footage for the episode was taken by March 2005, when one of my critical surgeries was filmed. The episode lasted a half an hour, although Nico and I were interviewed for about four hours. Pietra asked a variety of questions and I got the opportunity to tell her about many of the miracles. Sadly, by the final cut, I was given more credit than God. To everyone around me I gave the impression that I was satisfied with the finished product, but my heart knew that I should have done more to glorify God. Hence, this very book you're reading.

All the media attention did have a very important purpose. It helped facilitate yet another one of God's miracles.

MIRACLE NO. 17

Mr. David Gellar's outspoken criticism of the rear lap seat belt, coupled with all the media interest, made the authorities take notice. In late 2003 I was invited by the Land Transport Safety Authority to address the country's motoring chief executive officers on the extent of my injuries.

After my speech a vote was taken, and it was decided that all new cars entering New Zealand would have to comply with the amended safety law of over-the-shoulder rear seat belts. Although

New Zealand is still filled with secondhand imports with the fateful lap seat belt as restraint, I saw this decision as a major victory for our "cause": Making sure what happened to me did not happen to anyone else!

My pompous view of myself and how special I was for "deserving" all the miracles was an important phase in the making of 'the new' Ana. I needed to feel the guilt and the shame that resulted in my inaccurate estimation of myself. I needed to be humbled to get the facts reinforced: I was, am, and will always be a sinner unworthy of the grace and mercy God bestowed upon me! But...

They that be whole need not a physician, but they that are sick. But go ye and learn what that meaneth, I will have mercy, and not sacrifice: for I am not come to call the righteous, but sinners to repentance.

MATTHEW 9:12–13

FOOD FOR THOUGHT

The closer you get to God, the more humble you should be.

The closer you get to God, the less right you have to look down on people *you* deem as sinners. God is the only judge, and as his humble servant you should never lose sight of that.

When in doubt, study the life of Jesus. His humility should be an inspiration to us all.

SOUL SEARCHING

Have you ever experienced prejudice from someone near you because they deemed you to be less spiritual than they were?

How did you deal with the situation?

How do you think Jesus would have dealt with the situation?

Have you ever felt more worthy than a friend or family member of blessing because you saw yourself as closer to God?

What did God do to humble you?

CHAPTER TWELVE

And he said unto them, It is not for you to know the times or the seasons, which the Father hath put in his own power. But ye shall receive power, after that the Holy Ghost is come upon you: and ye shall be witnesses unto me both in Jerusalem, and in all Judaea, and in Samaria, and unto the uttermost part of the earth.

ACTS 1:7–8

It is of the LORD'S mercies that we are not consumed, because his compassions fail not. They are new every morning: great is thy faithfulness. The LORD is my portion, saith my soul; therefore will I hope in him. The LORD is good unto them that wait for him, to the soul that seeketh him. It is good that a man should both hope and quietly wait for the salvation of the LORD. It is good for a man that he bear the yoke in his youth. He sitteth alone and keepeth silence, because he hath borne it upon him. He putteth his mouth in the dust; if so be there may be hope. He giveth his cheek to him that smiteth him: he is filled full with reproach. For the Lord will not cast off for ever: But though he cause grief, yet will he have compassion according to the multitude of his mercies. For he doth not afflict willingly nor grieve the children of men.

LAMENTATIONS 3:22–33

TIMING

A MAN PLANS TO PROPOSE TO HIS GIRLFRIEND. HE WANTS TO MAKE IT AS romantic as possible. He drives her to a secluded beach, spoils her with a romantic picnic, and gets down on one knee. Let us assume two scenarios. This picnic takes place in the middle of the day and he pops the question directly after opening a bottle of champagne. Or, the picnic takes place at sunset and he pops the question just as the sun touches the sea on the horizon. Which proposal would be more memorable?

Your favorite baseball team has finally made it to the final playoffs. Once again, consider two scenarios. Your team claims victory due to a lackluster performance of their strong opponents. Or, your team hits a winning home run at the bottom of the ninth, after their opponents played the game of their lives. Which game would be more memorable?

The sunset proposal and the last minute home run would definitely stick around in my brain for longer. Why? The timing!

I want to use this chapter to demonstrate to you exactly how perfect God's timing is, and to do so I must take up my story in mid 2003.

As I explained earlier, my ileostomy bag was one thing I really struggled to get to terms with. Now, don't get me wrong. It is a wonderful product and millions of people worldwide either have colostomies or ileostomies. These bags serve an important purpose. There are many illnesses and cancers that make the use of this bag essential to the quality of life of so many people.

My problem with the bag was more related to the extent of my internal injuries than the bag itself. In the first two weeks after the accident, I had abdominal surgery on at least four occasions. I had three, initially four, fistulas oozing feces, and a tremendous amount of scar tissue. This, combined with my small intestine being ripped in a few places and the removal of my colon, meant that my digestive system had to evolve into functioning in accordance with the needs of my body. Initially, I could not handle food. The food that I did not throw up rapidly became fluid, and without the presence of a colon to help solidify it, filled my bag at an alarming rate.

I did have hope, though. I was told in the hospital that there was a possibility of having surgery to get rid of my bag as early as June 2003. I had an appointment with my surgeon, Prof. Martin, in mid-June. At that appointment he gave me the worst news possible. He strongly felt that I needed to have the bag indefinitely. He mentioned the tremendous amount of scar tissue. He was also uncertain whether my rectal muscles were able to function, as I was still paralyzed from the waist down. That news coincided with the news of Glenda's suicide and my depressive state. It was a major blow to me.

What do you think I did? What so many people do in similar situations? I blamed God! I conveniently forgot about all the miracles He had done in my life. All I could think of was how He let me down. I know! Pathetic, isn't it?

I felt myself become increasingly angry at God. I knew what He was capable of and I knew He could heal me. Why did He want me to wait? Did He not think I had suffered enough?

Three months later I once again saw Prof. Martin and he once again had the same prognosis. By now it was getting warmer and we were entering summer. This brought more problems to the table. Now, not only did my bag leak every couple of days, but the warmer weather meant I perspired more, and the skin around the opening of the intestine constantly became infected. The embarrassment of smelling bad all the time was now somewhat overshadowed by the pain of a sweat and stomach acid combination burning the skin on my abdomen. I became increasingly desperate to have my small intestine reattached the way nature intended.

My faith was really tested around this time. I constantly had to remind myself of all the good works God had done. I also had to work very hard at not resenting God for my predicament.

As with everything, if you allow God into a situation, and ask Him for a solution, He will not fail you.

What God taught me in those days was something all of us have heard before. There are only three answers to prayer: yes, no, and wait. Every time I brought up the subject of a reversal, I would be instructed to wait. God did this in various ways: through Scripture, through sermons, and also through the testimony of people with similar ailments. By March 2004 I was convinced that it was God's way of teaching me patience. I was blessed with so many instant miracles, I realized that He wanted to show me that some miracles take time. So I prayed and let God know that I realized what He was trying to teach me. I relinquished my will to Him and asked Him to schedule the surgery when He felt it would be most beneficial to my body.

I received an appointment with a new surgeon in June 2004. This surgeon had the news I was waiting for. He wanted to schedule a surgery for me in October or November of that year. The appointment with him though, was quite disconcerting.

He spent the whole time trying to talk me out of having the surgery. He told me that an alarming amount of people who have it wish they could return to having a bag. Apparently, the first year after the surgery is desperately difficult.

In essence, the surgeon fashions a "colon" with your existing small intestine. This is called a pouch. The reversal occurs in two separate surgeries, three months apart. The first surgery is to make the pouch from the lower part of the intestine currently unattached to the part protruding from the abdomen. The second surgery is to attach the intestine protruding from your abdomen to the newly formed pouch.

The surgeon warned me that in the first twelve months after the second surgery I would need to use the toilet between fifteen and twenty times a day. He also felt that I would have to wear adult nappies as my anal sphincters were not responding in the way they should. (Your internal and external sphincters are the muscles that control the movement of your anus.)

He explained that it took approximately a year for the new pouch to stretch sufficiently in order to morph into a colon.

Although all this information worried me, I still felt determined to have both surgeries and urged the doctor to schedule it. I was given a date in November.

Two weeks before the scheduled date, I was notified that the surgeon fell ill with some strange bug and all his surgeries had been postponed until January. I was very frustrated, but I knew that God was in charge. So, I literally bit my lip and braved another summer with the wretched bag.

January came and went. By mid-February I still had heard nothing from Middlemore Hospital. I was becoming a bit anxious. My mother flew out from South Africa in November to be there for the children during my recovery. As she is not a resident of New Zealand, she is not permitted to stay for longer than six months. In 2003 she stayed for a year, but only with special permission. She had to be out of the country by the end of April. Nico was also entering the Super 14 rugby season, which took him away from home for weeks on end. I desperately needed my mum around.

I contacted my ACC case manager and asked her if I could possibly have the surgery done by someone else. I explained my predicament to her and she approved funding to have the surgery done privately in Hamilton.

I now had to find a Hamilton-based surgeon. I phoned around and was given the number of a fellow South African, Dr. Dirk Drent. He was an urologist in private practice and I was confident that he could give me a good referral. Dirk, a fellow Christian with a heart of gold and a calling directly from the Big Man himself, referred me to David Schroeder. Mr. Schroeder is a surgeon who specialises in laparoscopic surgery and, in particular, laparoscopic stomach stapling. Dirk was very complimentary of David, and he assured me that David was an exceptional surgeon who has performed the rare type of surgery I needed.

Dirk got me in to see David the very next day. He was right! I could instantly sense that David was the man predestined to fix up the mess inside. He examined me and scheduled me in for the next week.

The surgery took place in a private clinic not far from my house. The procedure went well. It was major surgery and I only really felt the effects of the anesthetic wear off by day six after the surgery. I was discharged two days later.

The first two days at home were quite uneventful. I was very sore and very tired, as to be expected, but I did not feel too bad. Then, suddenly, the next day, I started vomiting. I could not stop vomiting. I dehydrated really quickly and was rushed to hospital. I spent the night in the emergency room receiving fluids and got discharged the next day. I felt a bit better, but I soon started vomiting again.

I could not get hold of Mr. Schroeder, as he was in Christchurch for a seminar. Dirk sent over his wife, Carien, to look in on me. She immediately sensed that something was seriously wrong with me and contacted David. He suggested I go back to hospital. Carien suspected that my wound was infected. While she was there, my wound felt very tender, but it did not have all the other telltale signs of infection.

I had to wait for Nico to get back from work to take me back to the emergency room. In the hours between Carien inspecting my wound and reaching the ER, my wound became very infected. By the time the emergency room intern examined me, the wound was oozing profusely. The doctor had no choice but to squeeze my skin, as you would a pimple, to press out as much puss as possible. A cup full of yellow, smelly, disgusting puss came out, and I had a hole the size of a tennis ball in my stomach. He cleaned it out, dressed it, and sent me up to a ward. I was to spend the next two and a half weeks in the hospital.

How did I react to this news? True to form, I started feeling very sorry for myself. I needed to undergo various tests in order for the doctors to ascertain the reason for my vomiting. I was taken off food and given an IV.

The one test I needed was to be done in radiology. To prepare me for the test, the nurses had to feed me a very disgusting fluid with a strange texture. The fluid illuminates during the test to show any possible leakages in my gut. This fluid also triggered some adverse response in my gut because it made my bag fill up at three times the normal rate. Before leaving for the radiology department, I already emptied the bag twice.

At Radiology I had to get another IV in my arm. The nurse took one look at my arm and knew that I had been a pin cushion for quite some time. When I told her of the origin of all the scars on my arm she felt relieved. She admitted to me that her first thought was that I was a junkie. It took quite a while for her to find a viable vein. During this time my bag filled up and I knew that it would shortly become critical that I empty it.

Now what do you think could make that situation worse for me? Let me tell you. First, get this mental picture in your head. I looked awful. Not only was I recovering from a surgery two weeks earlier, but I hadn't eaten in days. I was dehydrated. My lips were dry. My eyes were sunken in. I reeked. My hair was a mess. And in walks one of the most handsome men I have ever seen in my life. He was the radiologist on duty.

I had to tell him that I needed to empty my bag. I felt so embarrassed doing so. He told me that the test would not take long and that I should do it afterward. Part of the test was some procedure he had to do in my abdomen. I don't remember what it was; all I remember was that it was quite painful. After he did his bit and had all the tubes in place, he pushed me into the CT scan. The test was performed. The end of the test coincided with my bag bursting open and its contents leaking all over the slat I was on.

It was bad enough that my mum and my husband had to clean me up, but now this very attractive man had to do so too. On the way back to the ward I started crying. I cried! And I cried! And I cried! I think I probably cried for two weeks straight.

I did not cry because the man was attractive. I cried because of the humiliation. Although happily married, and not in the market for someone on the side, as a woman, I still had the need to retain some dignity around an attractive man. To me, that was the cherry on the cake of a horrible few weeks.

If there were an Olympics for self-pity, I would be the favorite to win gold. I sat in my hospital bed focused on poor old me. I tried to put up a brave face during visiting hours, but as soon as the visitors left, I threw my lip back to the floor.

I just could not make sense of it all. Why? Why, God, would you have me wait to have this surgery, just to see that I get this infection? How could you sit there and see me in misery and do nothing? What kind of a father are you? I could go on and on and on...

The scan revealed that I had a twisted intestine and that was the reason for my inability to keep food down. I had to remain on an IV until the intestine kinked itself right. That resulted in two and a half weeks in the hospital.

By the time I was discharged, it was already one month into my three-month waiting period for the second surgery. I was very weakened by not eating for so long and my focus for the next two months was to remain as healthy as possible. I took things very slowly at home and tried to stay in bed as much as I could. With a toddler and a five-year-old around, staying still in bed can be quite tricky. I was determined, though, to be healthy enough for the follow-up surgery.

The follow-up surgery was scheduled for the end of May. It was at the same clinic as before, and Mr. David Schroeder was going to perform it. In the months leading up to the second surgery, David and I spoke a lot about God, and David confided in me his faith in the Almighty. That gave me so much hope. It is wonderful to have a surgeon that is aware of more than the physical realm where science explains everything. I knew that David and I made a good team, and our combined faith would ensure a favorable outcome. I was right!

MIRACLE NO. 18

The procedure that I needed had only been done a handful of times in New Zealand. I was fortunate enough to have a surgeon who had done it successfully on a few occasions. Not only was he experienced in this type of surgery, but he was also prepared for any contingencies that could arise.

When he opened me up, though, something happened that even he could not predict. The pouch he formed three months earlier had filled up with 500 ml. of puss. When he cut into it, he had quite a hard time catching the entire amount of puss that oozed into the newly formed pouch. He was able to save the moment by thoroughly cleaning it out. He then cut out the source of the infection and pro-

ceeded to attach the two intestines together. Initially it seemed like human error. It was possible that he made a mistake in the first surgery that led to the infection spreading inward and not outward. This had serious implications for me. If the pouch had burst from all the puss, I could have died from the infection. It took a few days for us to realize that the building up off the puss was part of God's plan all along.

To test the success of the surgery, it had to be established as soon as possible whether I could use the toilet. The day after the surgery I felt the need to go and had a successful trip to the toilet. It was only two days after the surgery that we realized that I only needed to go between three and five times a day, as opposed to the fifteen to twenty times a day anticipated. Both David and I realized the purpose of the suffering of the past three months. The infection caused the puss to stretch the pouch. Under normal circumstances it takes a good year for the pouch to stretch sufficiently to only use the toilet five times a day.

God did reduce my "suffering" time. By evoking a few weeks of hardship, He prevented a whole year of potential humiliation and misery. Furthermore, my sphincter muscles worked from the very first day. I have never had the need to wear adult nappies.

God's timing is perfect. It's not always according to your way of thinking. It does not always fit into you life plan. But it is perfect!

FOOD FOR THOUGHT

Your life is predestined by God. He sees the big picture. Trust Him when obstacles look insurmountable. He *is* the light at the end of the tunnel!

God will reward your faithfulness with a miracle if you trust in Him. Although I felt sorry for myself, I knew in my heart that He was in control. It hurt Him tremendously to see me suffer the way I did. His heart went out to me. He knew what my body had been through, but

He also knew that it was necessary for me to suffer those two weeks in order for Him to facilitate His next miracle.

Modern life is all about instant gratification. If you have a problem, you want a solution as soon as possible. God does not work that way. He has solutions to all problems, but it occurs in His time frame. We don't always want to wait for Him to sort things out, but inevitably, in retrospect, it is always the best way to encounter and overcome difficulty.

SOUL SEARCHING

Have you ever been in a situation where you were forced to wait for God's timing to resolve a matter? What was it? How did it make you feel?

Is there a thing in your life at present that you could give to God to sort out in His own time? What is it?

Have there been instances in your life where you took things into your own hands, but in retrospect feel that it would have turned out more favorably had you listened to God's view on it?

CHAPTER THIRTEEN

"Thus, when you give alms, sound no trumpet before you, as the hypocrites do in the synagogues and in the streets, that they may be praised by men. Truly, I say to you, they have received their reward."

MATTHEW 6:2

HYPOCRISY

I PONDERED FOR A LONG TIME WHETHER I SHOULD PUT THIS CHAPTER IN the book. The truth is, I cannot omit it. There is an important lesson to be learned from the following experience.

The thing that happened next had a profound influence on my life. Three years on, and I am still living the consequence of it.

It was now June 2005. I was recovering from my long-awaited reversal surgery. I was basking in the joy of yet another incredible miracle. Nico was away on tour with a national team, a huge honor for him. Life was good! For the first time in two and a half years we could actually plan ahead. I was now walking again, my "plumbing" was sorted out, and I had all major surgeries behind me.

While I was in hospital, it was announced that an ex-rugby player, turned coach, was returning from a coaching stint in Europe. The newspapers announced that this man was to have the same job description as Nico. With obvious concern, Nico arranged a meeting with the head coach of the team.

To Nico, the head coach was not only his boss, but also his mentor. There are very few people that Nico really admired and looked up to, and this man was definitely one of them. Another thing Nico admired about him was his outward and outspoken faith in Jesus. The rugby environment is not always conducive to openly devout Christians. It has been said that rugby is a religion in New Zealand. There is a fanatical fan base. Young successful rugby players are not only thrust into the limelight, but have all the worldly distractions of fame, money, and groupies to contend with on a daily basis. So, if a man can sustain his faith in this environment, it is truly to be commended. This coach was like that.

A few days before his meeting, Nico received a job offer from a team in another country. He told the CEO of that union that he would get back to him as soon as he had the meeting with the head coach.

At the meeting with the coach, Nico urged him to be honest with him regarding his future. Nico told the man that he had another offer. Although he was not keen to take it up, he would, if the returning legend was to take his position. Nico trusted the head coach emphatically.

The coach reassured Nico that Nico's position as technical advisor was absolutely safe and that he was a valued member of the management team. Nico thus informed the CEO of the overseas team that he declined his offer. I was very relieved. I was too weak and too tired to even think of moving to another country.

That weekend I started noticing Nico's behavior as a bit strange. He worked long hours and I realized that with all the stress from my surgery and the two campaigns behind him, he was probably a bit burned out. He couldn't sleep. He hardly ate. He was visibly stressed. After this odd behavior escalated for ten days, I insisted he go and see a doctor. The doctor examined him, asked a few pertinent questions, and then referred him to a psychologist. The doctor suspected that Nico was suffering from posttraumatic stress.

On our way to the doctor, Nico got a phone call from the CEO of his current union. The CEO wanted to see him as soon as possible. I thought it a blessing in disguise, as I could ask the CEO if Nico could get a few weeks off to kickstart his recovery. We were on good terms with the CEO, but his demeanor immediately troubled me. He seemed nervous to talk to us. To me, that was very strange. He instructed Nico to come in the following day with a support person. He also mentioned that the union lawyer was going to be present. We immediately knew that it meant that Nico was probably going to be asked to leave.

We asked a dear friend of ours, Nico de Witt, to be our support person. Nico de Witt was a CEO of an engineering company and he knew the employment laws very well. At the meeting, Nico was told that he was being made redundant. Apparently there was no need for his expertise anymore.

To a man just diagnosed with posttraumatic stress, it came as a major blow. The layoff was not to be the most shocking event, though. What followed in the next few days thrust Nico in a very deep depression.

He had given five years to that union. He was very loyal and incredibly hardworking. When he got to the office the next morning to clear out his desk, the office lock was changed. His belongings were already put into a box and he was received with an icy reception. The man who took his place glared at us with contempt. It was a tremendously difficult day. Little did we know that it was about to get much worse.

Completely overcome by emotion, I sent the CEO a SMS message reminding him of whom he was dealing with. I told him that I defied logic by surviving a tremendous tragedy and that I was going to fight for my husband tooth and nail. I also sent photos of our children to any man I deemed to be part of the "conspiracy" of getting rid of Nico. In retrospect, I regret having my emotions taking over like that. It is not something I am proud of. I did not ask God how to handle it. I took matters into my own hands. For that, I feel ashamed.

It took Nico a few days to muster up the strength to unpack his box. When he did so, he made a startling discovery. Among the papers in his box was a columned outline in the head coach's handwriting. It was divided into three years: 2005, 2006, and 2007. In the column marked 2005, there were a few notes and the words "Nico Out." In the columns for 2006 and 2007, similar notes were made, but two other colleagues of Nico had the fateful word "Out" next to their names. Ironically, the man who had just taken Nico's job from him was also somewhere on that fateful list.

We decided to investigate the origin of this paper further and realized something that hurt me immensely. It seemed as if the outline had been made in late 2003. To me that was very significant. At that point I was still paralyzed, very ill, and weak. Our daughter was only three and our son a baby. The head coach was intimately aware of our circumstances. When he thus made these plans, he calculatingly knew that he was, in effect, going to put a man out of work who has a sick wife and two very young children. This head coach, this stellar servant of Christ!

Why do you think he would do such a coldhearted thing? Because he wants to be an "All Blacks" coach more than anything in the world. He was willing to step on anyone he deemed to be in his way.

The realization that this man was the one behind the betrayal literally crushed Nico and sent him into a downward spiral of severe depression. He had so much admiration and respect for this person. He revered the man's faith. He believed his coach when he said he loved God and Nico never anticipated that this man would be susceptible to becoming blinded by his ambition.

Nico was also hurt further when his work roles were only shuffled around. He was told that he was redundant. That was not true. The team manager wanted to create a position for his son and used this opportunity for nepotism.

Six weeks after my surgery, we found ourselves in a desperate situation. Our only bread winner was unemployed, distressed and totally despondent. He was not able to start working again, as his body completely collapsed. Nico started therapy and medication. It would be a long nine months before he could work again. We stared financial ruin in the face.

I realized something in those months. It is more challenging to be the partner of a depressed person that to be depressed yourself. When you experience feelings of depression, you have the power in your brain and in your heart to make a decision as to how you are going to deal with the feelings. You do have an element of control. When, however, you try to help someone else with depression, you don't have the luxury of choice. You can encourage, support, love, and pray as much as possible for that person, but the depressed one has to make the choice of rising above their circumstances themselves.

It was a profoundly difficult time for me. I so desperately wanted to help him. I so desperately wanted to take the hurt away. I so desperately wanted to make everything right. But it was out of my control. It was something that only God could do, with Nico as a willing participant. God could heal Nico, but all my faith meant nothing in that scenario. *Nico* had to believe that God wanted to heal his broken heart.

MIRACLE NO. 19

We were not completely without an income. We received income from the union for another few months. I started praying for money for when the income ceased. A few days before we were to receive the last amount, we received a check in the mail. It was from ACC. It was a compensation check. The amount was more than expected and it enabled us to survive the next six months!

"And why take ye thought for raiment? Consider the lilies of the field, how they grow; they toil not, neither do they spin: And yet I say unto you, That even Solomon in all his glory was not arrayed like one of these. Wherefore, if God so clothe the grass of the field, which to day is, and to morrow is cast into the oven, shall he not much more clothe you, O ye of little faith? Therefore take no thought, saying, What shall we eat? or, What shall we drink? or, Wherewithal shall we be clothed? (For after all these things do the Gentiles seek:) for your heavenly Father knoweth that ye have need of all these things. But seek ye first the kingdom of God, and his righteousness; and all these things shall be added unto you."

MATTHEW 6:28–33

FOOD FOR THOUGHT

It is important to have spiritual leaders and people to look up to. Don't ever forget, though, that the most important thing is your own personal relationship with Christ. People are human, and are all afflicted by the human condition. So, while it is good to have role models, place all the emphasis on God's Word, His truth and His love for you. That way the human iniquities and failures of those deemed "more holy" will not affect your relationship and view of God.

Too often people stray when a prominent "man of God" does something incomprehensible. The person failed you or your perception of righteousness, not God.

God is our Father, and as our Father He will take care of us, but there is a condition: "But seek ye first the kingdom of God, and his righteousness; and all these things shall be added unto you."

SOUL SEARCHING

Have you ever been hurt or betrayed by a person you revered as righteous? How did it affect your relationship with God?

Did you find it harder to forgive that person because you felt that they should know better? What brought you to the realization that that person needed forgiveness?

Have you ever been in an absolutely hopeless financial mess, just to have money arrive from an unexpected source at exactly the right time?

Chapter Fourteen

"Peace I leave with you, my peace I give unto you: not as the world giveth, give I unto you. Let not your heart be troubled, neither let it be afraid."

JOHN 14:27

"These things I have spoken unto you, that in me ye might have peace. In the world ye shall have tribulation: but be of good cheer; I have overcome the world."

JOHN 16:33

PEACE

PEACE IS PROBABLY ONE OF THE MOST MULTIDIMENSIONAL WORDS IN THE Bible. In the Old Testament, the word peace is mostly associated with war. In the New Testament, the apostles often used the phrase, "peace be with you," as a greeting. The most awesome reference to peace, though, belongs to *the man* himself: Jesus. When Jesus spoke of peace, he spoke of so much more than just our human understanding of the word.

We live in an age where most people have a therapist, or know a therapist, or have been to a therapist. After the accident, Nico, Trinita, my mum, and I spent some time with various therapists to work through the trauma of the tragedy.

Trinita suffered from night terrors after seeing all the blood at the accident scene. She worked with a psychologist to get her little brain around the events. Along with a lot of prayer, her night terrors subsided and she harbors no emotional ill effects.

Nico and I worked with a Christian therapist, Joan Morkel, for a few months. All this was around the time of my severe depression and suicidal thoughts. Joan's biblical and spiritual insight into the human heart was invaluable during this time.

I did have another therapist, though. Instead of paying this therapist, he paid me. In fact, I simply cannot put a price on what he paid me. He paid me with an unimaginable sacrifice: his life.

This is the story of how Jesus gave me peace. I don't have significant insight into the psychological workings of the brain. All I can offer you is my personal experience and my personal opinions regarding it.

I think one of two things seem to happen during a traumatic event. Your brain either shuts out all memories of the event, making you unable to remember anything. Or, it amplifies the memories to the extent that it almost seems like you are replaying it in "high definition."

The surviving member of the other car cannot, to this day, recall anything leading up to, during and directly after, the accident.

On the other hand, I can remember every minute detail of those fateful few hours. I do not only remember the physical events, I even recall all the smells, sounds, and tastes of the afternoon. My memories even circumvented all the morphine in my system. My last memory of that day was the face of the anesthetist directly prior to my emergency surgery.

Remembering everything in such detail meant that my brain would routinely bring those traumatic memories to the forefront—randomly during the day and also during dreams at night. This occurred mostly during my time in ICU.

The memory or dream was always the same. We were driving south toward Hamilton. It was hot. Christian was restless because his car seat caught the afternoon sun. There were cars everywhere. I looked up. I saw a little red car driving in our lane. After a second or two, I realized that the car was not going back into its lane and shouted out to Nico.

Then the impact! Then silence. Then the agonizing and frightened cry of two children!

Startled and with sweat on my brow, I would either wake up or shake the memory away.

It happened countless times in the first few weeks. It always coincided with the song that played on the radio at the time of the impact. I was definitely haunted by those memories, unable to stop them from hijacking my mind.

One evening, weak and too tired to fight the nightmare away, I prayed and asked God to take the memory away forever.

What do you think God did? No, He did not take the memory away.

What do you think He could have done to help me out? I'll tell you what He did. He turned the horrible reliving of a tragic event into one of my fondest memories! Right along with my wedding day and the birth of my children!

MIRACLE NO. 20

From that night onward, whenever I recall the accident, here is what I see:

We are driving south toward Hamilton. It is hot. Christian is restless because his car seat catches the afternoon sun. There are cars everywhere. I look up. I see a little red car driving in our lane. After a second or two I realize that the car is not going back into its lane and I shout out to Nico. My arms go out to brace my children. Then the impact! Then silence. Then the agonizing and frightened cry of two children!

Every time I see my arms going out to brace my children, I have a vision of a cross. My body position was that of a cross. I realized then that, had I braced myself, and not my children, I would have not been so extensively hurt. By bracing them, I inadvertently allowed the full force of the impact to rip through my body, but at the same time my actions kept them safely tucked in their car seats.

God showed me a passage in the gospel: John 15:13. "Greater love hath no man than this, that a man lay down his life for his friends."

Even today, I cannot recall the accident scene without seeing the cross and my body bracing my children.

By not erasing the memory, but by changing my perspective of the memory, God has turned it into one of my all-time favorite recollections.

I must stress, though, that I don't view myself as special or superior because of my actions that day. I did instinctively what any parent would have done if faced with a similar choice. I never gave my actions much thought. I held on to Trinita and Christian, and my well-being was the furthest thing from my mind. I love my children and I proved to myself that day that I was willing to lay my life down for my children. I also realized that if faced with a similar decision again, I would do the same. It gave me so much more understanding of the extent of Jesus' love for us. He loved us so much that being tortured and brutally murdered was a no-brainer to him.

Along with the revised version of my memory, God also gave me peace—a kind of peace that I find difficult to communicate to others. It's an inner serenity that I have never experienced before. It's an almost eerie calmness around the issue of the accident. It's an outright and wholehearted recognition of the consequences of the accident. It's the inner knowledge that the accident was merely a vessel in molding my spirit. All this has given me acceptance, and the acceptance has facilitated the peace. And it is truly a kind of peace that transcends all human understanding.

FOOD FOR THOUGHT

When something in your household breaks and is in need of fixing, the only logical thing to do is to send it back to its manufacturer. The manufacturer not only designed it, but also has the blueprints on how to fix it. Psychology and psychiatry are very useful sciences, and having made use of both, I will never devalue its importance in society. I do strongly feel, however, that one should always take the problem to the Manufacturer (God) first. If the manufacturer feels that a therapist might be helpful, then so be it. Only the manufacturer has the blueprint and the trouble-shooting manual to fix all the problems you may have.

SOUL SEARCHING

How has your brain responded to a past traumatic event?

What do you think is a better response to trauma: amnesia or detailed recollection?

Is there something in your life that could use God in the mold of a therapist? What is it?

Have you ever experienced true peace? When?

CHAPTER FIFTEEN

For thou hast possessed my reins: thou hast covered me in my mother's womb. I will praise thee; for I am fearfully and wonderfully made: marvellous are thy works; and that my soul knoweth right well. My substance was not hid from thee, when I was made in secret, and curiously wrought in the lowest parts of the earth. Thine eyes did see my substance, yet being unperfect; and in thy book all my members were written, which in continuance were fashioned, when as yet there was none of them. How precious also are thy thoughts unto me, O God! how great is the sum of them! If I should count them, they are more in number than the sand: when I awake, I am still with thee.

PSALM 139:13–18

LIFE

WHEN I WAS YOUNG, I LOOKED AT MYSELF AND MY ABILITIES AND SAW A future captain of industry. I was your typical run-of-the-mill type A overachiever who equated happiness with A plusses. At around age fourteen, I had my life completely mapped out. After graduating high school, I would go to a university and get a degree in organic chemistry. After which I would go to the south of France to a town called Grasse. There I would learn the ancient art of perfuming during the day while studying business practices at night. According to my projections, I would be a millionaire by age thirty, helping women across the globe to smell good.

That's what I saw when I looked in the mirror. That's not what God saw. God saw a mother.

Back then, the idea of being a full-time mum horrified me. I regarded it as a waste of a perfectly good brain. Being a housewife was definitely the very last thing I ever planned on being.

Even in my late teens, when I was forced to revise my long-term plan, I never saw myself as someone who would enjoy motherhood. Then, at age twenty six, I became pregnant.

TRINITA

I instinctively knew from the very beginning that I was expecting a little girl. I rushed to the mall and bought a little white dress with strawberries on it. The ultrasound confirmed her sex, and Nico and I eagerly awaited the arrival of our little angel in December of 1999.

As with all expectant parents, naming the baby was quite a big deal. Traditionally, one would name the child after their parents. I really wanted to honor my parents and parents-in-law in that way, but I also had the overwhelming desire to honor my heavenly Daddy too. I decided that I would name all my children after God first, and then after an earthly parent, second. With Trinita it came easily. My maiden name was Trindade, which means Trinity. I looked the word up in an Italian dictionary and saw the word Trinita. With that name not only do I indirectly name her after my earthly father, but I acknowledge God every time I call her. What could be better than that?

She was born at 6:04 A.M. on the fifteenth of December. When the gynecologist put her on my chest, any and all previous hopes and dreams faded into the oblivion. I was instantly smitten, and in that second realized that there was only one thing I wanted to be more than anything else—a mother.

She weighed 3.4 kg., was 54 cm. tall and got 10 out of 10 for her AGPAR test. She was perfect. The only unexpected thing about her was her hair color. It was an intense shade of mahogany. Although my mother was a redhead, I always envisaged my children differently. I had never seen such a beautiful color in my life!

Trinita was a joy to parent from day one. She was a very good baby. She hardly ever cried, even when she fell or bumped her head. As a toddler, her personality began to take shape. I realized that she was definitely a social butterfly. She craved interaction with her peers from about eighteen months and hasn't parted with her social flare since. She loves people. She is kind and gentle, albeit a tomboy. She is sweet and caring. She is smart and inquisitive. She is adventurous. She is beautiful. Her most valuable trait, though, comes directly from God: she is strong. In the past six years there have been so many times where her inner strength and conviction has left me in awe. She experienced so much pain and separation and trauma and chaos. Yet, she would routinely display wisdom beyond her years when faced with an obstacle.

Trinita changed my destiny. She is my daughter. She is my hope. She is my hero.

CHRISTIAN

Christian's conception was completely unexpected. We were in New Zealand for less than a year. We were experiencing financial hardship. The thought of having another mouth to feed terrified me. I truly believed that the timing of his arrival was not good. In fact, I only really came to terms with the pregnancy in my third trimester.

By that time we knew that it was a boy. As with Trinita, I wanted to name him after God and a grandparent. My father-in-law was named after a historical figure of the Anglo Boer War, Christiaan de Wet. We decided on Christian.

Christian was born at 3:20 A.M. on the eleventh of December 2002. He weighed 3.2 kg. and was 54 cm. tall. I had a water birth with him. Just prior to his arrival, Tracy, my midwife, informed Nico that he was in actual fact going to bring Christian into the world. She calmly instructed him on what to do. He caught Christian, cut the umbilical cord, and held onto him while Tracy took care of the afterbirth. The experience was so meaningful to me because I knew how much I cherished those first moments with Trinita. Now Nico had an opportunity to bond with his son!

I instantly fell in love with Christian. Knowing that it took me some time to accept his arrival, I vowed to make up for it by being the most loving and accepting mother I could be. At that time I did not know that I would only have less than four weeks with him. If I did, I would have poured a year's worth of hugs and kisses into those precious few weeks.

The main thing the accident robbed me of is the first year of my son's life. I cannot quantify the amount of tears I have cried because of my absence in his first twelve months. Most of my anguish in the hospital was the result of knowing that other people were raising him, and not me.

MIRACLE NO. 21

Many child development experts may not view this as a miracle, and may feel that it does happen under certain developmental circumstances. I, on the other hand, know in my heart why it happened.

Christian started walking at the age of eight months and seven days, on the eighteenth of August.

At that time all I craved was a relationship with my baby. I felt so far removed from him. There were countless times where I looked at him and he felt like a stranger to me.

The only way he could come to me is if someone brought him over. I was still bedridden and very weak. As soon as he could walk, he could come over to me all by himself, and he did.

We fell in love with each other all over again, and God cultivated a relationship between mother and son that nothing could break.

Today, we have a great relationship. He adores me and I him. We are very close and not one day goes by without him telling me the words I thought I'd never hear from him: I love you, mamma.

In certain respects he is so different from Trinita. Where she has strength beyond her years, he has a sense of humor beyond his. He makes us laugh! His big blue eyes are alive with mischief and fun. He is smart. He is spontaneous. He is energetic and vibrant. He is sweet and caring, but everyone knows that he only gives hugs and kisses to his mum. And I adore that about him.

Christian changed my destiny. He is my son. He is my hope. He is my sunshine.

MIRACLE NO. 22

Many of you might have pondered why I have not yet included their survival of the accident as a miracle. Good observation!

To me, it is the ultimate miracle! So much could have gone wrong in those auspicious few seconds.

Not only did I brace the children, but God cradled them in His hands. They were completely unhurt. They literally got away without a scratch.

The reason I have only brought up this miracle now is because I wanted to put emphasis on the miracle of life in general. This miracle had to coincide with their "beginnings," because when they read this someday, I want them to know that to me, their survival is a miracle, just like their birth, every breath they take and every day they enrich my life with their presence.

"Thou didst knit Trinita and Christian together in my womb. We praise thee, for thou art fearfully and wonderfully made."

FOOD FOR THOUGHT

Find a resource at the library, book store, or Internet about conception and the nine months following it. Read up about it. Ponder the miracle of life and how significant you are to God. Wow!

You are intrinsically part of God's plan. Long before your grandparents were even born, God already planned your arrival on earth. He already loved you and believed in your abilities. You are fearfully and wonderfully made and you do have a purpose!

SOUL SEARCHING

Think back to your ancestors and their lives. Ponder how many things had to fall in place to have you conceived. Try and comprehend how very important you are to God. Make a commitment to love yourself as God loves you.

If you are a parent, how has it changed you?

What life lessons have you learned by observing and also interacting with your children?

How has parenthood affected your relationship and understanding of God?

CHAPTER SIXTEEN

DEATH

I WAS GIVEN A SECOND CHANCE AT LIFE. IN THE PAST SIX YEARS I HAVE become increasingly aware of the value and the meaning of life. I have also become very appreciative of bodily functions that one never really gives much thought to.

Every day when I get up and walk somewhere, I truly appreciate the functioning of my legs. Although I have not regained complete sensation, I am able to walk quite comfortably with the aid of a splint.

I also have a greater understanding and respect for the human digestive system. For the best part of two years I had to experiment with different foods to determine whether my new gut could handle it. Subconsciously, I am aware of the effect of everything I put in my mouth.

I am truly in awe of the human body. My body was forced to withstand tremendous pain and trauma, and not only has it overcome the stress, but it has taught itself to function in spite of it.

The news is not all good, though. There was a casualty in the accident. Something did die—my sensuality.

As you know, the accident occurred only twenty-six days after my having natural childbirth.

Giving birth is an extremely traumatic event for the body. Although women are designed to do this, bringing life into the world through a tiny space takes its toll. Not only are women really fatigued the first six weeks after labor, but they often still bleed. Many have stitches from where they tore. If the physical repercussions are not enough, our hormones pretty much go into fifth gear. We are susceptible to postnatal depression. If we are able to sidestep the depression, the fatigue—brought on by a lack of sleep—often leaves us weepy.

In essence, my body was still recovering from all this when tragedy struck.

Not much thought was given to my reproductive system during

my stay in hospital. There were so many other pressing matters to attend to. About six months after the accident, Nico and I attempted to make love. It was incredibly painful and he could not penetrate me at all. I was referred to a gynecologist for tests. An ultrasound and an internal examination revealed that my uterus collapsed onto my vagina. There were significantly less intestines to "fill" up my insides. With an absent colon and seriously compromised abdominal muscles, the uterus basically kept on dropping until it came to rest on my vagina. This basically meant that penile penetration was not possible until further surgery could reconstruct my insides. This procedure was to be done in conjunction with the fashioning of the j-pouch. It meant that we were physically unable to have sex for two and a half years.

For the first eighteen months, it was not really an issue in our marriage. I was still very weak and my damaged nervous system made me hypersensitive to any kind of touch. Even a strong breeze on my legs would send me through the roof with pain.

Nico was the most understanding and supportive husband in the world. He never put any pressure on me and constantly reminded me that he was happy that I had survived.

I had so much emotional and physical healing to do that I failed to really notice that I had absolutely no libido. I guess a part of me believed that my sexual drive would return once my vagina was surgically restored.

It didn't.

Doctor David Schroeder was the surgeon responsible for the surgery. During the same procedure he made me a pouch that was going to take up the role of a colon. The surgery was a triumph. Our next attempt at lovemaking was successful. Although the angle of the vagina was slightly altered to what it was previously, lubrication and penetration became possible. I still experienced pain as a result of nervous system regeneration, but I was able to reach orgasm, something I was not sure would be possible after severing my spine.

It was now almost thirty months after the accident. I was able to, finally, make love to my husband. Yet, it was the last thing I wanted to do. When we did make love, it was more out of duty and guilt. I felt like I was failing him on so many levels. I just hated having sex.

I could not understand why. I knew of many women who were unable to reach orgasm, yet they still enjoyed sex. Here I was, able to reach satisfaction quite easily, but I had no need to be intimate.

The more the other parts of my body recovered, the more I became aware of my lack of craving sexual intimacy.

I hated being naked. I could not look at myself when I was naked. I felt repulsed at myself. When I looked in the mirror, I would get physically nauseated.

I couldn't understand it. I knew I wasn't disgusted by my scars. I loved my scars. I really looked at them as battle scars. In summer I always wore shorts and skirts, not concealing my scars, but proudly showing them off.

I could not understand why I had completely lost my sensuality, and it caused a lot of distress in my heart.

Needless to say, it started taking its toll on our marriage. Nico was not satisfied with our physical relationship. Unfortunately, his own depression led him to believe that I was rejecting him and not myself. He finally spoke out about it in the spring of 2007.

I assumed for so long that he was dealing with our lackluster sex life, so that when he told me that he was desperately unhappy, I became determined to get to the bottom of this phenomenon. I needed to know why I didn't feel like a woman anymore!

Our first appointment was with a doctor specializing in sexual problems. Although she could not help us, the meeting with her was quite insightful. She told us that male sexual problems are much easier to fix. There is a series of medication available for men experiencing a lack of libido. Female sexuality, on the other hand, is a much more complex issue. There is no simple tablet that can be taken to remedy the matter.

After a background check, the doctor told us that she was not at all surprised that I had no libido. There are a range of things that negatively influence female sex drive: trauma, stress, pain, and the hormonal repercussions of childbirth. All of the above was experienced by me during a short space of time. Within twenty months of immigrating, I gave birth and suffered unimaginable trauma with the accident. For quite some time after the accident, sex and pain were synonymous to me.

She tried to put both of us at ease by explaining to Nico that it was not a reflection on him, and that I should not be so hard on myself. She also suggested that we see a psychologist that specializes in sexual malfunction.

I left her office feeling quite dejected. I really wished for there to be a tablet or capsule that could make me feel like a woman again. I was really worn down by the guilt of not being a good wife to my husband and also the feelings of inadequacy within myself around being a sensual creature.

I so craved to feel the warmth and excitement of sexual arousal. I so longed to just be sexy and feel sexy and do sexy things.

But, I just felt that it was not something to go to God with. (It doesn't make sense, I know. After all, God invented sex!) I just never wanted to bring this problem to Him. I felt too ashamed. It's thus no surprise that it was the only major issue still unresolved after the accident.

Nico and I started seeing Leena St. Martin, a sex therapist. I was very sceptical going into the meetings. Up to that point I had just utilized Christian therapists and I was not sure whether her input or viewpoint would complement mine. Desperate for an answer, though, I attended all the sessions.

During our fourth session, Leena made a startling observation. As you may know, oftentimes in psychology the explanation for deviant or inexplicable behavior can be put down to some kind of trauma that one's "inner child" is responding to in a negative way.

Leena reminded me that in 2003 I had, for all practical purposes, all the needs of an infant. I needed to be carried to the toilet. I needed help showering. I soiled myself. On occasion, I would even wet the bed. I was completely incapable of doing things that any healthy and normal thirty-year-old woman would regard as part of her daily routine. Her opinion around my self-repulsion was that I sexually regressed to childhood. As it's not natural for a young child to have a sex drive or need of sexual intimacy, I responded in that way.

Her explanation made sense to me. I also suspected that my injuries played a part too. I felt that the damage to my nervous system could also have suppressed sexual arousal. Now, my task was to follow her instruction on how to regain my sensuality.

Every week she would give me "homework" to do. Most of it revolved around becoming more aware of me and my identity as a woman. I diligently did all she asked and reaped the benefits. By the end of December, I started seeing myself as a sexual being again. Viewing myself in that way also slowly restored my libido.

I was so excited. At this point I had already started writing this book and I was convinced that 2008 was going to be the best year I'd had in six years.

Christian was due to start school in February of 2008. With him away from home for thirty hours a week, I could concentrate on finishing this book. Nico and I were also looking into starting a business together. He was between rugby contracts and it was the perfect time to start something that could provide a backup income, as rugby can be an unforgiving profession. The idea of working so closely with him was very exciting. It was an opportunity for us to cement our strengthening relationship! 2008 was going to be my year!

CHAPTER SEVENTEEN

Put on the whole armour of God, that ye may be able to stand against the wiles of the devil. For we wrestle not against flesh and blood, but against principalities, against powers, against the rulers of the darkness of this world, against spiritual wickedness in high places. Wherefore take unto you the whole armour of God, that ye may be able to withstand in the evil day, and having done all, to stand. Stand therefore, having your loins girt about with truth, and having on the breastplate of righteousness; And your feet shod with the preparation of the gospel of peace; Above all, taking the shield of faith, wherewith ye shall be able to quench all the fiery darts of the wicked. And take the helmet of salvation, and the sword of the Spirit, which is the word of God: Praying always with all prayer and supplication in the Spirit, and watching thereunto with all perseverance and supplication for all saints; And for me, that utterance may be given unto me, that I may open my mouth boldly, to make known the mystery of the gospel.

EPHESIANS 6:11–19

WARFARE

Many Christian denominations either try to avoid the above words as far as possible or downplay the role Satan plays in trying to ruin our lives every day. The truth is we are in a spiritual battle every minute of every day, whether we dispel Ephesians 6 or not. Our battle is not against flesh and blood!

In early 2008 it became frightfully clear: my battle was "not against flesh and blood, but against principalities, against powers, against the rulers of the darkness of this world, against spiritual wickedness in high places."

By the turn of the New Year I had already written six chapters. I was a bit apprehensive about writing chapter seven and eight because it meant reliving the most emotionally traumatic part of my ordeal. So, when I decided to take January and most of February off and enjoy the summer in South Africa with our family, it was partly out of spending quality time with them, but mostly out of fear. The subject matter for chapters seven and eight was the first six months after my release from Middlemore hospital. It was an incomprehensibly difficult time for everyone in our situation. I wanted to portray the events as accurately as possible, but that meant revisiting all the painful memories.

I realize now that a lot of that fear was instilled by Satan because "God has not given us a spirit of fear but of power and of love and of a sound mind."

I was finally ready to start writing again by the end of February. The children and I returned from South Africa on the twenty-third. Nico had to remain there for a further two weeks. We were researching purchasing a South African franchise. He also spent the time networking, as he had formulated a very profound and an all-encompassing rugby training course for children.

Trinita and Christian started school on the twenty-fifth of February. I was hosting guests who had just emigrated from South Africa. I was excited about my return home because I had not known Debbie and Wouter long before we invited them to stay with us. I so looked forward to fostering a new friendship with them. Wouter was Nico's childhood friend and I viewed his presence in Nico's life as precious. Nico had suffered a lot with depression and posttraumatic stress. Having an old friend around to bond with was a great comfort to me.

During the first week in March, it became evident that Satan was not going to make the writing and releasing of this book easy for me.

From the minute that I was aware of God's role in my miraculous recovery, I dreamed of writing a book to tell the world about our wonderful, faithful, and loving God. I knew that I needed to glorify Him and in doing so help thousands of other people to realize how precious they are and how much God loves them. I wanted to tell the world that miracles happen every day to everyone!

Two days prior to Nico's return to New Zealand, he phoned me and asked me a question that not only profoundly stunned me, but caught me completely off guard. He told me that he wanted me to tell him whether we should end our marriage or not by the time he got back. I was speechless. The last encounter we had was a loving one at the airport. We were both cautiously enthusiastic about a possible business purchase and the embarking of a new adventure. After years of me avoiding sexual intimacy, we were finally, in my mind, on track to a "happy ever after." His question ripped the rug out from under me.

The next day I got a severe anxiety attack (an occasional occurrence since the accident). I went to the doctor to get some prescription medicine to slow down my racing heart. There, I broke down in tears. Dottie, our GP, had known us for seven years. She was the one who initially diagnosed Nico with depression. She reminded me that it could be the depression speaking. At that point, although we were embarking on a new business venture, Nico was unemployed. A month earlier he was offered a contract with a South African union, but a contractual agreement could not be reached and the offer fell through. She was of the opinion that he was simply very stressed out and not thinking clearly. After speaking to her I felt calmer and realized that he might be more optimistic once home and surrounded by his loved ones and possessions.

That was not the case.

The man who returned from South Africa was not the man I greeted at Johannesburg airport two weeks earlier. Something drastic must have happened to him, because he had changed completely. I noticed it in the way he looked at me. With disdain and anger!

His strange demeanor continued well into April. He often pressed me for an answer to his question. He wanted to separate.

Of course, with all this going on in the house, the writing of this book completely halted. For the following five months Nico and I were embroiled in a battle to either save or end our marriage.

I now look at the irony of it and smile, but at the time it was not humorous at all. I was putting off writing chapters seven and eight because of the emotional trauma connected to it. Yet the hurt that I suffered between April and July of 2008 was frightfully similar to the pain of April to October 2003.

We endlessly debated separation and/or divorce. Initially I was dead set against it. I believed that whatever was troubling Nico could be overcome. We fought every day. We were hurtful to each other every day. We had become enemies.

I eventually decided that I would file for divorce. A lot happened between us that I am not willing to discuss in this forum. I do, however, want to share why I had reached my decision.

My husband was desperately unhappy with our marriage. I realized during that time that his relapses into depression were solely rooted in his search for fulfilment in our relationship. I had told myself for a long time that it was due to the accident or work pressure, when indeed the "blame" was to be put squarely at my feet.

The accident changed me. In the previous chapter, I discussed the sexual ramifications of the accident. That was not all that changed.

My whole outlook on life, how I approached problems, how I raised my children—everything was irreversibly and radically changed. For the most part, all personality modifications were very positive. I do think, though, that Nico felt like he did indeed, after all, lose me on the fifth of January 2003.

The new Ana Marie became almost invincible. I became so intrinsically aware of my inner strength and faith in God that I perhaps didn't need my husband as much as I used to. I became assertive and independent, something I definitely was not prior to '03. I also displayed a level of confidence not dependant on my appearance, but rather on my character.

These traits are not negative traits, but when your life partner changes so radically, it can be quite daunting. Nico felt that I didn't need him anymore. His feelings of inadequacy were also pronounced by my lack of libido. I think he craved to have the old Ana Marie back.

That is why I filed for divorce. I could not go back to who I was. I liked the woman I was now. I didn't want to change back and I didn't feel that God wanted me to change back.

It is often said that if you love someone you should set them free, and if they return, it was meant to be, or something to that effect. That quote haunted me throughout our struggle to save our marriage—with one difference: I knew that I could not let him come back, even if he wanted to.

I know that some who may read this will disagree with my decision, but each of us has to do what we feel is the right thing according to our circumstances. Unless you are living someone else's life every day, it is hard to discern his or her decision. (or "fully comprehend" his or her decision)

Although the breakdown of our marriage had been incredibly hurtful, I can with sincere conviction and transparent intention inform you that I want nothing more than for Nico to be happy. I want him to find the woman who can lift him up and complete him on every level.

I am to this day convinced that no other man could have supported me and guided me through the tragedy as he had. I also owe him my life. I am certain that his prayers directly after the accident, were absolutely, irrefutably responsible for my survival. His prayers put God's plan of miraculous intervention into action!

Are you still sceptical about our struggle being against the rulers of the darkness? What happened to me in 2008 just goes to show that Satan plays dirty.

I was in the process of writing an account of God's wonders, and in Satan's desperation, he turned my marriage into a battlefield. He attacked my marriage. A marriage that wasn't perfect, but consisted of a lot of love!

You may argue that it is not fair to blame Satan for problems within my relationship. I know, however, that he is solely to blame. The reason I know that is rooted in Ephesians 6.

As part of my daily prayer I always ask God to protect us with His full armor, in body, mind, and spirit. I know how important it is to have the belt of truth buckled around your waist, to have the breastplate of righteousness in place. I also know how crucial it is to have your feet fitted with the readiness that comes from the gospel. Not the mention, to have on the shield of faith and the helmet of salvation. Furthermore, I try to quote a few crucial memory verses as part of my "sword of the spirit."

I do this all, because in my near-death experience Satan was there accusing me. I realized then how fundamentally essential it is to be spiritually protected.

Please realize that putting on this armor does not mean I don't sin. I wish it did. I am still ashamedly a very sinful person. I make mistakes every day. I do things daily that need repenting of.

It does mean, however, that I am protected. In turn, that means it's harder for Satan to attack me. So he attacked the person closest to me. He attacked the love of my life.

Had this all occurred a few months earlier, Satan would not have been able to get his claws into Nico. Nico diligently put on his armor every day. During our time in South Africa, however, he experienced some spiritual reservations, which in turn gave Satan a gap. He filled Nico's mind with so many lies and his heart with so much hurt. So, when Nico returned, it was no wonder he lashed out in the way that he did.

The reason the marriage ended is very personal. The breakdown of our marriage was incredibly painful and it incited many feelings of shame, disappointment and inferiority. For a long time I struggled with the emotional and spiritual repercussions. God has been faithful though in healing my heart. He pointed out scripture that helped me make peace with the decision. He showed me that I did not disobey him by getting a divorce. He helped me heal.

Make a joyful noise to the LORD, all the lands! Serve the LORD with gladness! Come into his presence with singing! Know that the LORD is God! It is he that made us, and we are his; we are his people, and the sheep of his pasture. Enter his gates with thanksgiving, and his courts with praise! Give thanks to him, bless his name!

For the LORD is good; his steadfast love endures for ever, and his faithfulness to all generations.

PSALM 100

FOOD FOR THOUGHT

From the moment we are born, we are on trial for our lives. Satan is the prosecutor. God is the judge and Jesus is the defense attorney. Every time we sin, we give the prosecutor leverage in his case against us. Jesus' death radically affected these court proceedings. Now, every time we sin and repent it, that sin becomes inadmissible in court.

SOUL SEARCHING

To what extent do you believe Satan has an effect on your life and your choices?

Have you ever experienced spiritual warfare?

Do you put on the full armor of God? How has it changed the way you make decisions and deal with concerns?

CHAPTER EIGHTEEN

Praise the LORD. I will give thanks to the LORD with my whole heart, in the company of the upright, in the congregation. Great are the works of the LORD, studied by all who have pleasure in them. Full of honor and majesty is his work, and his righteousness endures for ever. He has caused his wonderful works to be remembered; the LORD is gracious and merciful. He provides food for those who fear him; he is ever mindful of his covenant.

He has shown his people the power of his works, in giving them the heritage of the nations.

The works of his hands are faithful and just; all his precepts are trustworthy, they are established for ever and ever, to be performed with faithfulness and uprightness. He sent redemption to his people; he has commanded his covenant for ever. Holy and terrible is his name! The fear of the LORD is the beginning of wisdom; a good understanding have all those who practice it. His praise endures for ever!

PSALM 111

WISDOM

Lessons I Have Learned

But the fruit of the Spirit is love, joy, peace, patience, kindness, goodness, faithfulness, gentleness, self-control; against such there is no law.

GALATIANS 5:22–23

A LOT OF THE THINGS I HAVE LEARNED THROUGH IT ALL ARE THINGS I already knew, but never literally experienced. So, a lot of what I am about to relay to you may sound either obvious or elemental, and not necessarily that profound, but please bear with me. Please try to ponder these truths and make them your own.

145

My first lesson was that God loves me. He loves me with a supernatural kind of love that transcends the manmade laws of science and physiology. He loves me so much that He witnessed the death of His own child in order for me to be saved. If not for Christ, there would not have been a discussion between God, Satan, and me during my near-death experience. It would simply have been me and Satan discussing some logistical issues surrounding my eternity.

God's love is so real, so pure, so all-encompassing, it surpasses our understanding. Humans can simply not fathom the depth and utter comprehensiveness of God's love for us.

His love comes with a great big dollop of faith in us too. He is God. He is omnipresent, omniscient, and almighty. He created everything. It would have been so effortless for Him to create us without giving us our own free will. It would have made life much easier for Him. Yet, His love for us was unselfish. He loved us enough to give us a choice to love Him in return. To me, that is not only a sign of His faith in us, but also His respect for us.

My third lesson was that bad things do happen to good people. It does not for one second mean that God loves you any less. It does present you with more opportunity, though, to experience His love for you even more. When you are at your weakest, God is at His strongest. He will maneuver and plan and manipulate situations in order to help you; all you need to do is ask.

I also learned that merely asking is not enough. You need to believe that what you have asked for will happen. Hebrews 11:1 says: "Now faith is the assurance of things hoped for, the conviction of things not seen." You need to be spiritually convinced that something will happen, even if it seems unlikely in the physical realm.

In saying that, another lesson has been that I need to do my bit too. I learned that faith is not only believing, but actively seeking and responding. Although I believed that God healed my legs and that I would walk again, I actively participated in the physiotherapy. I did what needed to be done in the physical realm to accelerate my healing.

I feel it is not only a way of being in partnership with God, but also an acknowledgement that He is doing wonderful works in your life.

After witnessing firsthand how awesome God's works are, I have come out the other end a much more positive person. The pre-2003 Ana Marie was a glass-is-half-empty kind of person. If I could draw something negative out of a situation, I did. Now, I view everything as positive. Hardships are seen as opportunities to grow. Challenges are viewed as character builders. I have completely shifted my paradigm of happiness and contentment. All because I know God is in charge and I wouldn't want it any other way!

The power of prayer is another thing that has left me dumfounded. It is something, I regretfully confess, I have sorely underestimated, most of my life. I have always prayed, for as long as I can remember. One of my earliest memories is of me saying my bedtime prayer as a little girl. Maybe due to its habitual nature, its true impact was underestimated. So I urge you: never, ever, make the same mistake as I did. Never underestimate the power of prayer!

A lesson that has profoundly impacted my daily life is the principle of praising God. I have learned that you can never in a million years say thank you enough to God for everything He has done for you. When and where I can, I say thank you. Not because He expects it, but because He deserves it. Praise God every day, whether it is in song, or with words or by actions. Just let Him know you are grateful. Praise Him even more during difficulties. It activates His "rescue" plan!

They say patience is a virtue. I think it's one of those virtues that you don't really appreciate, unless you have it. I was an impatient creature—in everyday situations as a parent, as a daughter, as a wife. I got annoyed quite easily. It had to be my way or the highway. I have grown more patient through the tragedy, but even that is God's "fault." I learned that His timing is perfect. This is something that was learned after a long, delayed, and impatient wait. After waiting and being blessed with yet another miracle, I realized that there is not much point to impatience. God's timing is perfect, so why rush things? It's a life principle that has trickled down to everyday situations. The result: a more patient, and consequently, better to live with, person.

I also attained inner peace. It's something that eluded me all my life. To be able to feel an inner peace every day, even in difficult situations, is absolutely priceless.

I still have all the usual human emotions. I still feel emotional hurt and rejection. I still get angry and annoyed. I still feel sadness and pain. The inner peace God has given me, though, transcends all those negative emotions. I do feel all those things, but it pales in comparison to the contentment and acceptance inner peace allows me to have.

The two people who probably benefit the most from all the lessons learned after the accident are my children. I believe in my heart that it has made me a better parent, in so much that I don't take any single day with them for granted.

I urge you: tell your children that you love them and appreciate them every single day. Tell them that you accept them and love them unconditionally. Tell them that you are grateful God gave them to you. Teach them about Jesus!

Yes, they will still disobey. Yes, they will still do things that annoy and even embarrass you. They will probably still try to rebel. But the knowledge that you love them no matter what will go a long way in their understanding of God's love for all. Remember, how you love your children is how they will learn to love others, including God.

Another lesson I have learned is that of humility. We live in a society where gaining celebrity status is the dream of so many people. When God came to earth, though, He did not choose to be born in a castle fit for the Prince of Peace. He was born in a smelly, unhygienic, cold, and totally unimpressive stable. From Jesus' very first breath he was humble. Everything about his life screams humility. That very fact should prevent us from elevating our own personal status. But we don't. Our need for self-actualization and peer recognition thwarts any attempt to be unassuming. Many times, without even being aware of it, we get a little above our station.

Humility, in my opinion, is a learned trait. It is a trait one can choose to adhere to. Why is it so important to be humble? Because you are absolutely nothing without God! Everything you are, everything you do, every breath you take, every thought you have—nothing would be possible if God did not create you.

The final lesson I learned was not to take myself too seriously. Prior to the accident, I was unable to laugh at myself. I think it was a combination of two things: a jaded sense of humor and a need to be significant. Finding my own faults and mistakes comical was simply not an option. At first, losing many of my bodily functions made being able to laugh at myself critical for self-preservation. I had to chuckle if I fell over or my bagged leaked.

Initially, I used humor to merely take the edge off the seriousness of the situation. One day I heard someone say, "Take God seriously, but don't take yourself too seriously." I decided that that was not a bad suggestion and have since tried to adhere to it.

Now don't get me wrong. I am not humble all the time. I am not peaceful all the time. I am not calm and collected all the time. I am definitely not obedient all the time. In fact, I am a shameful sinner with many faults. I often do things I regret. I often say things I regret. I am so far from being the perfect follower of Christ, it's scary. I can say, however, that I try very hard. I acknowledge that I am only human. I acknowledge that I am fallible. I acknowledge that I am nothing without God!

My goal is to live by Galatians 5:22–23: "But the fruit of the Spirit is love, joy, peace, patience, kindness, goodness, faithfulness, gentleness, self-control."

And in doing this, I hope to honor God.

In Conclusion

I DON'T KNOW ABOUT YOU, BUT I HATE UNHAPPY ENDINGS. WHEN I WATCH a movie or read a book where the main character dies or doesn't get the girl, I get very annoyed. There should always be a happily ever after!

For that reason I found it hard to end this book. When I started writing it, I had a happy ending all mapped out. I never anticipated the demise of my marriage while completing my testimony.

I simply did not know how I was going to finish it off without readers thinking, "Well, that horrible! She got hurt, got better, and then got divorced!"

For months I mulled it over in my mind. How was I going to "spin" this? I was sad, on the edge of a matrimonial split, and absolutely financially broke. I started convincing myself that no one would want to hear (and believe) the testimony of someone as down and out as I was.

I believed that God's miracles in my life would only impact readers if my life turned out perfect.

I was wrong, again.

MIRACLE NO. 23

Writing this book! It is miracle number 23. I had a desire to write an account of the accident for many years. Once again, God's perfect timing came into play. Telling you my story, sharing with you all of God's wonderful works in my life and how He can impact yours, was all part of His plan for my life, all along.

The writing of this book became one of His healing tools in my heart.

Its significance is twofold:

By retelling every detail I was presented with an opportunity to gain a clearer insight into my heart and all the pain that had not yet been assimilated. Through my testimony, God's gift to me was closure.

Secondly, He knew that it would be best for me to write the book while in the turmoil of ending my marriage—although, it did not make sense to me at first!

Those of you who have been through a traumatic divorce know that some of the overwhelming feelings are that of loneliness, rejection, and failure. By writing this story during these dark times, God was reminding me of some impenetrable truths every single day:

I am not alone. I am never alone. He is always with me. He is my Father, my protector, and my best friend.

He will never reject me. "For I am sure that neither death, nor life, nor angels, nor principalities, nor things present, nor things to come, nor powers, nor height, nor depth, nor anything else in all creation, will be able to separate us from the love of God in Christ Jesus our Lord" (Romans 8:38–39).

And...

I am not a failure to God.

He used this book to heal my broken heart.

Finally, He showed me that there is something just as appealing as a happy ending...and that is a new beginning. That's where I am at!

Now may the God of peace who brought again from the dead our Lord Jesus, the great shepherd of the sheep, by the blood of the eternal covenant, equip you with everything good that you may do his will, working in you that which is pleasing in his sight, through Jesus Christ; to whom be glory for ever and ever. Amen.

HEBREWS 13:20–21

ACKNOWLEDGEMENTS

Nico, Ma, and Daddy
Trinita and Christian
Ma Magda and Pa Chris
Kenny, John, Ronny, Carlos, and their families
Teresa and Melanie
    and
Shelly and Aidan
My extended family
All my dear friends (you know who you are)
Stephan Joubert
Every person who prayed for us during that critical time
The paramedics, fire service, and police officers at the scene. In particular the paramedic who escorted me on the helicopter. Unfortunately I don't know your name, but you are always in my thoughts.
Lorraine Abrahams
Wayne Waysee
Meesah Geary
Sergeant Gregory Waters: Thank you for your thorough and comprehensive crash scene investigation.
Sergeant Mark Toomey and Ngari: Thank you for handling our case with so much empathy and relentless diligence—which even included bringing the children toys!
The Huntly Police Department
Professor Martin and Mr. Adams and all your theater staff: I have not yet met Mr. Adams to thank him personally, but wish to do so someday.
Mr. Gellar: He is truly incomparable—not only in his extensive knowledge of trauma, but also his whole demeanor. It sounds strange, but he brought light and color to the ICU with his presence. He is remarkable!
All the Middlemore ICU staff: in particular Rinah and Julliette

All the staff, nurses, and nurses-aids from Middlemore Hospital Ward 19: in particular the charge nurse, Reti, Shandra, Mark, John, and Huco.

All the nurses and nurses-aids from Middlemore hospital's Ward 20 under the leadership of Chantal. Chantal, you were superb! You went out of your way to support my emotional needs. Thank you.

Thank you also to Edgar, Erica, Jessi Jenny H., Jenny D., Desiree, Ancy, Andrea, Christine, Denise, Pamela, Richie, Buelah, Karin, Lisa (for the foot rubs), Robin, Paula, Shelley, Mala, Celter, Melissa, Hayley, Lisea, Nishi, Waina, Jeni, Sandra, Robin, Maree, Riza, Oyodette. and all the other nurses and staff who took care of me in Ward 20.

Helen from Ward 20 admin: thank you for your friendship and going the extra mile for me.

Sandra, Titus, Marius, and Bernard

Graham

Kerry

The physiotherapists: Sheralata, Jos, Lucy, and Maree

All my occupational therapists

The staff of the Otara Spinal Unit

Trinita's kindergarten teachers at North Harbour Preschool

Hamilton's South African community

Claire Lua

Renie Neale

Panacea Healthcare

The staff at Pharmacy 547: in particular, Neville Puckey who delivered pain medication to my house at one in the morning! How's that for service?

Everyone at Davies Corner Accident and Medical

Dr. Dottie Prinsloo

Dr. Noel Choonoo

The Waikato Hospital Emergency Department

The surgeons and specialists at Anglesea Clinic in Hamilton

Mr. David Schroeder

Dirk and Carien Drent

The Waikato Hospital Ward 2 nurses: in particular Dilgah and Maria

Mr. John de Waal

The North Shore and Hamilton Southern Cross hospitals

Joan Morkel

Christine Voster

Leena St. Martin

Geoff Garton

All the staff at Westminster Christian Preschool and Primary School

I am sure I have neglected to mention someone. It is merely because I have been overwhelmed by the love and support of countless people. I therefore thank every person who has touched my life since the fifth of January 2003.

There are two very important institutions that need a wholehearted thank you: ACC and WINZ

The Accident Compensation Corporation of New Zealand (ACC)

ACC is a New Zealand government-run insurance company specializing in all kinds of accidents at home, at school, at work, and on the road.

ACC has paid for everything! This includes three months in the hospital, comprehensive rehabilitation, fifteen surgeries, and expensive medication. ACC has also footed the bill for a nanny for Christian for three years and reconstructive surgery on my leg and abdomen.

There are a myriad more things I have been covered for by ACC. Their care has been extraordinarily comprehensive.

I wish to thank my lifetime planner Rayna Nielsen and all my ACC case managers.

My greatest gratitude goes to the New Zealand government for the heartfelt care of their citizens! Thank you New Zealand for ACC!

Work and Income New Zealand (WINZ)

WINZ is another New Zealand government agency that proved to be invaluable. It is the unemployment agency for the country.

There were times that we were in dire need of their financial assistance. For that I am eternally grateful.

When Nico and I separated, however, their aid stepped up a notch. I was offered counseling for myself and the children to help us deal with the breakdown of the marriage. Due to the fact that I was a stay-at-home mum with altered physical capabilities, WINZ set about in helping me to find a suitable career. I was thoroughly tested and great effort was made to find me a "dream."

Thank you Maria, Courtney, Michaela, and Carol: You have treated me with so much dearness and respect during a very difficult time in my life.

Thank you WINZ for being a safety net for people experiencing hardships.